D1073384

CONTENTS

Introduction	4
Chronology	7
Design and Development	9
Technical Specifications	17
The Strategic Situation	24
The Combatants	31
Combat	49
Statistics and Analysis	75
Aftermath	77
Further Reading	79
Index	80

INTRODUCTION

The Spitfire and the A6M Zero-sen were two fighter aircraft with amazing similarities. Both saw their major combat debut in 1940 and both quickly achieved an almost mystical reputation as deadly aerial fighting machines. Indeed, the two types famously made critical contributions to the winning of key campaigns – the Spitfire during the Battle of Britain and the Zero-sen during Japan's lightning conquest of Southeast Asia at the start of the Pacific War.

SPITFIRE VC
VS
A6M2/3 ZERO-SEN

Darwin 1943

PETER INGMAN

OSPREY PUBLISHING
Bloomsbury Publishing Plc
PO Box 883, Oxford, OX1 9PL, UK
1385 Broadway, 5th Floor, New York, NY 10018, USA
E-mail: info@ospreypublishing.com
www.ospreypublishing.com

OSPREY is a trademark of Osprey Publishing Ltd

First published in Great Britain in 2019

A catalogue record for this book is available from the British Library.

ISBN: PB 9781472829603; eBook 9781472829610; ePDF 9781472829597;
XML 9781472829627

19 20 21 22 23   10 9 8 7 6 5 4 3 2 1

Edited by Tony Holmes
Cover artwork and battlescene by Gareth Hector
Three-views, cockpits, Engaging the Enemy and armament scrap views by
Jim Laurier
Maps and formation diagrams by Bounford.com
Index by Fionbar Lyons
Typeset by PDQ Digital Media Solutions, Bungay, UK
Printed in China through World Print Ltd.

Osprey Publishing supports the Woodland Trust, the UK's leading woodland
conservation charity.

To find out more about our authors and books visit **www.ospreypublishing.
com**. Here you will find extracts, author interviews, details of forthcoming
events and the option to sign up for our newsletter.

Acknowledgments
The author gratefully acknowledges assistance provided by Bob Alford,
Peter R. Arnold, Langdon Badger, Michael Claringbould, Tony Cooper,
Yasuho Izawa and Andrew Thomas.

Spitfire VC cover art
On 15 March 1943 the first sustained combat between RAAF No. 1 Fighter
Wing Spitfire VCs and 202nd Kokutai A6M2 Zero-sens took place over
Darwin. The latter were escorting a force of 'Betty' bombers from the 753rd
Kokutai that were flying at their usual high altitude of 23,000ft. With no time
to form up as an entire wing, several loose formations of Spitfires climbed
independently to meet the intruders. One of these groups comprised seven
No. 54 (RAF) Sqn Spitfires that were bounced out of the sun by Zero-sens. In
the ensuing dogfight, Flg Off Al Mawer got onto the tail of an A6M2 and shot
it down from close range – FPO2c Seiji Tajiri was killed. The wingtip of
Tajiri's fighter was recovered from Darwin Harbour and duly became a
No. 54 Sqn trophy. (Cover artwork by Gareth Hector)

A6M2 Zero-sen cover art
During the attempted interception of the Zero-sens and 'Bettys' over Darwin
by No. 1 Fighter Wing on 15 March 1943, the unit's Wing Commander
(Flying), Wg Cdr Clive Caldwell, was absent and the wing was instead led into
action by No. 452 Sqn's CO, Sqn Ldr Ray 'Throttle' Thorold-Smith in
BS231. A seven-victory ace from his time serving with the unit in combat on
the Channel Front in 1941–42, Thorold-Smith led a ragged line of Spitfires in
a determined but foolhardy attack on the high-flying 'Bettys' that were in turn
fiercely protected their Zero-sen escorts flying above the bombers.
Unsurprisingly, Thorold-Smith was shot down, although his machine
remained undiscovered until 1986, resting on the bottom of Darwin
Harbour's West Arm. The loss of the popular and experienced squadron leader
was keenly felt by No. 1 Fighter Wing, and it was speculated that his
decision-making was adversely affected by a lack of oxygen in the minutes
prior to his death. (Cover artwork by Gareth Hector)

Previous Page
Flt Sgt C. R. Duncan of No. 452 Sqn waits at readiness with his Spitfire at the
airstrip on Milingimbi Island in November 1943. Fighter detachments were
regularly maintained at this isolated location to the east of Darwin, although
there were no further Japanese raids on the island after 28 May 1943. Months
earlier, Flt Sgt Duncan had been forced to bail out of a Spitfire during the
30 June raid on Fenton, his aircraft being one of seven Mk VCs lost on this
date. (AWM)

A duel between the Spitfire I and the A6M2 during this early war period would have been a fascinating prospect for aviation enthusiasts. While this never happened, Spitfire VCs of No. 1 Fighter Wing, Royal Australian Air Force (RAAF) did meet Zero-sens of the Imperial Japanese Navy Air Force (IJNAF) during the 1943 dry season campaign over Darwin in northern Australia. While an improvement on the Mk I, the Mk VC was still sufficiently close to the original Spitfire design to be a reasonable match for the Zero-sen. As will be seen, the results of this campaign were perhaps surprising, and a product of many contributing factors, some of which have been topics of much controversy since the end of the war.

Aside from the three units that made up No. 1 Fighter Wing (Nos. 452 and 457 Sqns (RAAF) and No. 54 Sqn (RAF)), two other RAAF squadrons flew the Spitfire VC. No. 79 Sqn deployed to Goodenough Island, off the eastern tip of New Guinea, in June 1943. Despite being just 400 miles from the major Japanese stronghold of Rabaul, the unit had a relatively quiet time in respect of aerial combat and did not meet a single Zero-sen during several months in the area. No. 85 Sqn operated Mk VCs from September 1944 until the end of the war, although it remained exclusively in Western Australia all this time and never encountered the enemy.

Where else might the Spitfire and Zero-sen have met in combat? Three Royal Air Force (RAF) units – Nos. 136, 607 and 615 Sqns – flew Mk VCs in Burma from late 1943, and they narrowly missed seeing combat with A6Ms that were escorting bombers during a raid on the Indian city of Calcutta on 5 December 1943. This attack was most unusual because it proved to be the only time IJNAF fighters escorted Imperial Japanese Army Air Force (IJAAF) bombers during the entire Burma campaign. Most of the time the Spitfire's adversaries in-theatre were IJAAF Ki-43 'Oscar' and Ki-44 'Tojo' fighters.

From early 1944 fighter squadrons in Burma began re-equipping with Spitfire VIIIs, which were vastly superior to the Mk V in respect to their performance. Mk VIIIs also subsequently served in the Netherlands East Indies (NEI), although there was little chance pilots flying these machines would engage Zero-sens in combat by this late stage in the conflict. Details of these campaigns can be found in *Osprey Aircraft of the Aces 87 – Spitfire Aces of Burma and the Pacific* by Andrew Thomas. In 1945, carrier-based Seafires, developed from the Spitfire, saw combat against A6M5s off Japan, as chronicled in *Osprey Duel 16 – Seafire versus A6M Zero* by Donald Nijboer.

So, the only sustained combat between the Spitfire V and A6M2 Zero-sen took place over Darwin in 1943. At that stage of the war, the IJNAF still had a strong cadre of experienced pilots, although they were steadily being diluted owing to growing attrition in combat. They faced a group of Australian and British pilots led by Wg Cdr Clive Caldwell, the leading Australian ace of the war and the highest-scoring P-40 pilot of any nationality.

Because of the geographical isolation of Darwin, the two combatants – No. 1 Fighter Wing and the 202nd Kokutai – would meet each other repeatedly, and largely without prospect of intervention by other fighter forces. During the 1942 bombing campaign in northern Australia, after some initial reverses, Japanese pilots had developed tactics such as flying at high altitude that resulted in not a single bomber being lost to defending United States Army Air Force (USAAF) 49th Fighter Group

LEFT
A trio of pilots from No. 54 Sqn practice formation flying near Sydney in January 1943 prior to moving north to Darwin, where all three aircraft were to be used to claim victories. Nearest is BS164/K, in which Sqn Ldr Eric 'Bill' Gibbs made all of his claims (five and one shared victories and five damaged). Next is BR544/A, which Flt Lt Robin Norwood was flying when he was credited with shooting down a Zero-sen on March 15. The third Spitfire VC is BR539/X in which Flt Lt R. W. 'Bob' Foster made most of his claims (three destroyed, one probable and two damaged). (Ralph Murphy)

(FG) P-40 Warhawks for several months. However, flying at greater ceilings would offer no protection from the Spitfire VC, which gave its best performance at such high altitudes. The Commonwealth pilots flying the aircraft in the defence of Darwin entered battle confident of a decisive victory.

JAPANESE TERMINOLOGY

The IJN's terminology used in this volume should be applied as broad guidelines only, and there are no exact Western equivalents. Confusion often arises with these terms, because the IJNAF used a complicated parallel organisational structure with terminology to match. Some terms refer to personnel within an administrative framework, which was firmly established, and others reflect tactical and operational aircraft formations. To confuse matters further, some of the terms listed here cover both aspects:

Kokutai – an IJN air group, consisting of between three and six chutai

Hikotaicho – commander of a kokutai

Chutai – a sub-unit of nine aircraft

Chutaicho – leader of a chutai

Buntai – equivalent to a chutai, but usually accompanied by administrative or established command status

Buntaicho – leader of a buntai

Shotai – a tactical formation typically of three aircraft (although sometimes two or four aircraft)

Shotaicho – leader of a shotai

Sentai – an operational formation of IJN warships (not be confused with the IJAAF term for an aerial formation, or hiko sentai)

JAPANESE RANK ABBREVIATIONS

FPO1c   Flying Petty Officer First Class
FPO2c   Flying Petty Officer Second Class
FPO3c   Flying Petty Officer Third Class
Sea1c   Seaman First Class

CHRONOLOGY

1940

10 July to 31 October — Battle of Britain is fought and won by the RAF. The Spitfire I is largely tasked with taking on Luftwaffe fighters – a role it performs superbly.

13 September — In China the Mitsubishi A6M2 makes its combat debut when 13 Zero-sens engage 30 Republic of China Air Force (RoCAF) Polikarpov I-15 and I-16 fighters near Chongqing and give them a severe mauling. The IJNAF pilots down 13 RoCAF aircraft without loss.

1941

10 September — The 3rd Kokutai is re-organised as a fighter unit equipped with A6M2 Zero-sens.

8 December — The 3rd Kokutai flies the first long-range fighter escort mission from Formosa to Luzon. In a series of IJNAF raids, the United States Army Air Corps (USAAC) in the Philippines suffers severe losses.

1942

January – February — The 3rd Kokutai ranges over the NEI and destroys dozens of Allied aircraft during a series of successful long-range missions.

19 February — Darwin is devastated during a massive raid by more than 200 aircraft from four aircraft carriers and two land-based bomber kokutais.

3 March — Nine A6M2s of the 3rd Kokutai launch a devastating raid on Broome from Koepang, on the island of Timor, 600 miles away. Twenty-three aircraft (including a number of seaplanes) are destroyed.

8 March — Following the surrender of the NEI on this day, the 3rd Kokutai can now largely concentrate on missions over Darwin.

30–31 March — First clashes between 3rd Kokutai A6M2s and 49th FG P-40Es over Darwin.

April — The 49th FG succeeds in shooting down nine Takao Kokutai G4M 'Betty' bombers during daylight raids over Darwin.

28 May — Prime Minister Winston Churchill agrees to send three Spitfire squadrons to Australia.

May – August — Peak of 1942 dry season campaign. The 3rd Kokutai increases Zero-sen escorts and no further 'Bettys' are lost to 49th FG P-40Es.

June — During a brief attachment to the Kenley Wing, Wg Cdr Clive Caldwell flies Spitfire VBs over France and learns 'Balbo' tactics.

August September — First six Spitfire VCs arrive in Australia. A 3rd Kokutai detachment is sent to Rabaul to assist with Guadalcanal operations.

7 October — No. 1 Fighter Wing formally raised at RAAF Base Richmond, made up of Nos. 452 and 457 Sqns (RAAF) and No. 54 Sqn (RAF). Caldwell is made Wing Commander (Flying) three months later.

1 November — The 3rd Kokutai is redesignated 202nd Kokutai.

1943

January — Spitfire VCs make 2,000-mile ferry flight from Sydney to Darwin.

February	No. 1 Fighter Wing takes responsibility for air defence of Darwin.	**30 June**	First attack on Fenton airfield, south of Darwin. Seven Spitfires lost.
6 February	No. 54 Sqn shoots down a Ki-46 'Dinah' reconnaissance aircraft for No. 1 Fighter Wing's first aerial victory.	**6 July**	Second attack on Fenton airfield, and another seven Spitfires are lost.
		18 July	No. 457 Sqn shoots down a 'Dinah', killing both crew. One of the latter is Capt Shunji Sasaki, CO of the 70th Dokuritsu Hiko Chutai.
2 March	First clash between No. 1 Fighter Wing and the 202nd Kokutai during a low-level Zero-sen raid on the airfield at Coomalie Creek, south of Darwin.		
		13 August	'Bettys' revert to night raids.
		17 August	Four 'Dinahs' are downed by No. 1 Fighter Wing.
15 March	First interception by Spitfires of 'Bettys' with Zero-sen escorts over Darwin.	**7 September**	Last Spitfire versus Zero-sen combat.
		27 September	Last Zero-sen mission over Australia, when four A6M2s escort 21 IJAAF Ki-48 'Lily' bombers in an attack on Drysdale Mission and airfield in Western Australia.
2 May	Controversial large scale combat in which 14 Spitfires are lost, some after running out of fuel.		
10 May	First strafing attack on the airstrip on Milingimbi Island, 270 miles east of Darwin.		
28 May	Second Milingimbi attack, and four 'Bettys' are lost.	**11 November**	'Betty' shot down by No. 457 Sqn at night, resulting in cancellation of Japanese offensive missions over Australia
20 June	Only IJAAF raid on Darwin.		
28 June	Darwin raid by 'Bettys', with Zero-sen escort.		

An A6M2 Zero-sen of the 3rd Kokutai at Lakunai, Rabaul, in September 1942. It was this unit, renumbered as the 202nd Kokutai, that fought so effectively with Spitfires over Darwin in 1943. Note the width of the fighter's rugged landing gear, which allowed the Zero-sen to operate safely from the rough landing fields of the NEI. (Tony Holmes Collection)

DESIGN AND DEVELOPMENT

During 1940–42, the Spitfire and the Zero-sen were the stand-out fighters of the European and Pacific theatres, respectively. Both became known as agile, high-performance aircraft that were feared by their adversaries. However, each came from opposite ends of the design spectrum. The Spitfire was a short-range defensive interceptor, while the Zero-sen was intended for long-range offensive missions.

The Vickers Supermarine Spitfire traced its lineage back to a private initiative by its designer, Reginald J. Mitchell, following which the Air Ministry subsequently wrote a formal specification around the aircraft. Prototype K5054, which flew for the first time on 5 March 1936, featured streamlined stressed-skin construction, a retractable undercarriage and, eventually, an armament of eight 0.303-in. Browning machine guns. The latter were mounted within the aircraft's distinctive elliptical wings and fired from outside of the propeller arc, thus avoiding the need for a synchronising mechanism and the complications that were associated with such devices.

No. 54 Sqn Spitfire VC AR564/DL-L over typical northern Australian terrain, its now-famous elliptical wings (a major factor in the aircraft's excellent performance characteristics as a fighter) being clearly visible from this angle. The unit's 'DL' fuselage code differed from the 'KL' codes it had long used when based in Britain. Flt Lt Robin Norwood may have had some influence in this choice as his wife's two given names were Dorothy Langridge. (Ralph Murphy)

Arguably the two standout features of the Spitfire prototype were its engine and wing. The Rolls-Royce PV-12 installed in K5054 evolved into the exceptional Merlin that proved capable of being developed into successively more powerful versions of the same basic engine. The elliptical wing shape helped give the Spitfire its characteristic appearance. Engineered primarily to fit the eight machine guns stipulated by the Air Ministry specification, it so happened to be one of the best fighter wings of its era. Indeed, during World War II Spitfires proved capable of sustaining dives of Mach 0.9, which was faster than that achieved by some early jet designs.

While Britain possessed a potentially world-beating fighter design in the late 1930s, it proved difficult to adapt the Spitfire's advanced stressed-skin design to mass production techniques. This in turn meant that the Vickers Supermarine aircraft was slow to enter service in quantity and was greatly outnumbered during the Battle of Britain by its less glamorous counterpart in Fighter Command, the Hawker Hurricane. In January 1942, it was Hurricanes that were rushed to the Far East and saw combat against IJAAF and IJNAF fighters and bombers as the latter swept all before them in the skies over Singapore, Java and Ceylon. Only in 1943 were Spitfires finally available to defend northern Australia.

The Mitsubishi A6M Zero-sen, meanwhile, was born from an IJNAF specification to replace the Mitsubishi A5M carrier fighter. Featuring stressed-skin construction like the Spitfire, the A6M was among the first mass-produced fighters to feature wing-mounted cannon in the form of two Type 99-1 20mm weapons. Although capable of inflicting considerably more damage than rifle-calibre machine guns, the Type 99-1 possessed a slow rate-of-fire and a low muzzle velocity, which reduced the weapon's effectiveness in aerial combat. The Zero-sen prototype first flew on 1 April 1939 – a full three years after the Spitfire. It showed exceptional performance characteristics, although the definitive A6M2 design did not emerge until December of that year in the form of the third prototype.

Spitfire VC EE853 (A58-146) on display at the South Australian Aviation Museum in Adelaide. This example was recovered from New Guinea (in 1973 by Langdon Badger), where it had served with the RAAF's No. 79 Sqn until written off in a landing accident in August 1943. However, it is identical to the Mk VCs that flew with No. 1 Fighter Wing over Darwin that same year. Note the barrel for the single 20mm cannon protruding from the port wing (a second cannon could be housed in the stub alongside it, although Spitfires flown in Australia had only a single 20mm weapon per wing) and the two ports further outboard for the 0.303-in. machine guns. (Author's collection)

SPITFIRE VC

29ft 11in.

11ft 5in.

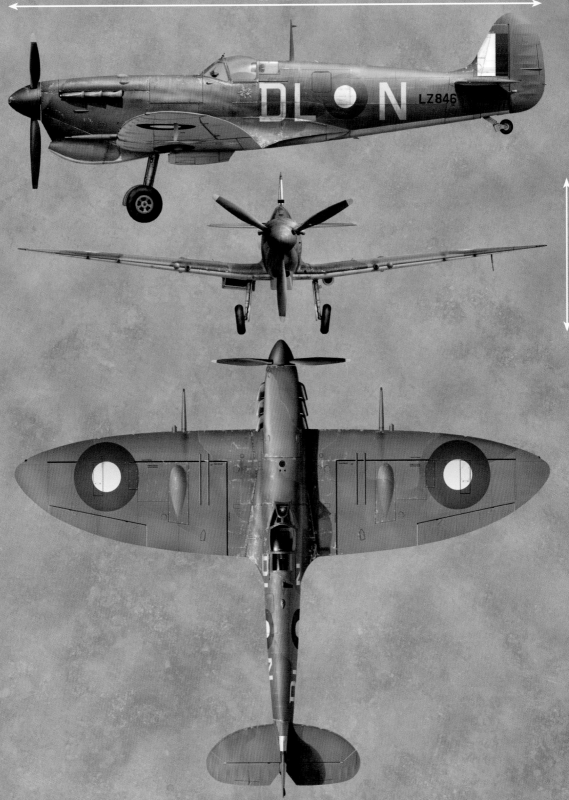

36ft 10in.

Japanese aircraft and weapons were given a numerical type designation related to a particular year in the Japanese calendar. 1940 was the Japanese year 2600, and so the A6M2 was officially known as the Type 0 Carrier Fighter Model 21. In Japanese, its popular name was Rei-sen – 'Zero-fighter' when translated into English. In 1942 the Zero-sen was given the Allied codename 'Zeke', and both were used interchangeably in combat reports from then on. However, the name 'Zero' was widely used during the war, and remains better known today.

Because of its lightness, the Zero-sen achieved good performance despite its Nakajima Sakae-12 radial engine generating a relatively modest 950hp. Many sacrifices were made to keep the weight down, with the A6M2 lacking both armour plating and self-sealing fuel tanks. It also carried just 60 rounds for each of its 20mm cannon. Because of these choices, and thanks to the installation of a 150-gallon internal fuel tank that could be augmented by a droppable 94-gallon external tank, the Zero-sen boasted an unmatched endurance when it entered frontline service with the IJNAF. However, it was a very finely balanced aircraft. Any increase in weight would significantly degrade its performance and range.

The original Spitfire I was comparable to the Zero-sen, as its Merlin III engine produced 1,030hp. Many upgrades were made to the design within a short time, including an increase in protective armour for the pilot, metal instead of fabric-covered ailerons and a metal variable-pitch propeller in place of the original fixed wooden Watts airscrew. The net result was additional weight that would have decreased performance had it not been for progressive increases in the power output of the Merlin engine. A key feature of the Spitfire's airframe was that it was able to absorb these numerous changes, which in turn meant it was the only British fighter to remain in production throughout the entire war.

The Spitfire VC was the model that fought in the skies over Darwin in 1943. The Mk V was the most numerous of all the Spitfire variants built, although by 1943 it was already being superseded in most theatres by the superior Spitfire IX. Numerous improvements meant that the Mk V was more than 500lb heavier than the original Spitfire I. The 'C' in VC referred to the 'universal' C-type wing that was designed to reduce manufacturing time and allowed for three different armament options. The 'C' wing featured either eight 0.303-in. machine guns, two 20mm cannon and four 0.303-in. machine guns or four 20mm cannon. Early-build Spitfire VCs were delivered with four 20mm cannon, but two of these weapons were usually removed once the fighter was in frontline service. Later, production would shift back to the B-type wing of two 20mm cannon and four 0.303-in. machine guns. The Spitfire Vs that fought over Darwin in 1943 were fitted with B-type wings, despite being designated Mk VCs.

The Australian aircraft were powered by Merlin 46 engines rated at 1,210hp on take-off. Crucially, this version of the Rolls-Royce powerplant boasted a single-stage supercharger optimised for high-altitude performance. This meant the Mk VCs gave their best performance at altitudes exceeding 18,000ft thanks to the generation of an extra 200hp by the supercharger.

The RAAF aircraft are sometimes further specified as being Spitfire VC Tropicals, which refers to modifications intended to suit operations in the demanding northern Australian climate. Most obvious of these was the provision of a Vokes filter, which prevented excessive dust entering the engine. Fine dust was an engine killer, for sand

entering the Merlin caused excess wear, lower power output and a shortened lifespan. To battle the dust the Vokes filter was added. Housed in a beard-like faring under the fighter's nose, it was not popular with pilots. While the filter reduced the Mk V's top speed, its benefits far outweighed any reduction in performance caused by excessive wear.

When the RAAF first flight-tested its Mk VCs near Sydney in late 1942, it was believed they were up to 20mph slower than earlier standard Spitfire VA/Bs. The Vokes filters were blamed, but subsequent tests proved they only had a marginally negative effect on performance. The actual cause of the poor performance was more complex, being related to the Merlin 46s only generating their maximum output at high altitude. Actual experience in Darwin would soon put these concerns into perspective, as differences in performance between individual aircraft could be even more significant, depending on a variety of factors such as airframe age, engine wear and maintenance history.

Other tropical items were also added. Fitted in the rear fuselage behind the cockpit was a tank for 1.5 gallons of drinking water, along with a container of flying rations, an emergency tool roll, survival equipment and a signal pistol with cartridges.

The original A6M2 model of the Zero-sen, fitted with the 950hp Sakae-12 engine, was the variant that enjoyed so much success during 1940–42. The Japanese commenced production of the improved A6M3 in early 1942, the aircraft being

On 27 December 1942, this A6M3 of the Tainan Kokutai was found abandoned at Buna airstrip in New Guinea by advancing Allied troops. Built by Mitsubishi in June of that year, the fighter was adorned with the Kanji subscript Hokuku – 870 (Ko Gen), indicating that this fighter had been donated by a civilian volunteer group possibly from occupied China. It was subsequently shipped via barge, along with parts from five other A6M3s found at the site, to Eagle Farm in Brisbane, Queensland, in February 1943. The aircraft was returned to airworthiness by TAIU-SWPA personnel through the incorporation of missing parts obtained from other abandoned Zero-sens at Buna. (NARA)

A6M2 ZERO-SEN MODEL 21

28ft 8in

X-102

10ft 0in

39ft 4.7in

The Buna A6M3 was briefly test flown from Eagle Farm following a six-month rebuild that saw parts from six Zero-sens combined to make one airworthy aircraft – the fighter is seen here in flight off the Brisbane coast in August 1943. By the time it flew trials against a Spitfire VC (which confirmed the superior manoeuvrability of the Japanese machine), the comparative performance of the two types was already well known following several months of hard-fought combat. Among the changes introduced with this version of the Zero-sen were squared-off wingtips that improved the fighter's roll rate and speed in a dive (AWM).

powered by the improved Sakae-21 that featured a two-stage, two-speed supercharger that increased the engine's output to 1,130hp. However, the modifications needed to accommodate the longer and heavier Sakae-21 (specifically a new cowling with a revised carburettor air intake) meant that endurance and manoeuvrability were sacrificed for only marginal improvements in speed, aileron control, roll rate and performance in high-speed dives. The A6M3's lateral control was achieved by eliminating the wing-folding mechanism and fairing over the wingtips, shortening the wingspan by almost three feet and reducing the span of the ailerons. Codenamed 'Hamp' by the Allies (the aircraft was originally given the codename 'Hap', but after intervention by the Commanding General of the USAAF, Gen Henry 'Hap' Arnold, it was changed to 'Hamp'), no A6M3s were ever encountered over Darwin, owing to the variant's inferior range when compared to the older A6M2.

So how did the Spitfire VC Tropical compare to the Zero-sen? This can be answered with some authority following comparative flight testing between the two types that took place in Australia in August 1943. The Zero-sen in question was an A6M3 'Hamp' that had been found abandoned at Buna airstrip in New Guinea by advancing Allied troops on 27 December 1942. Assigned to the Tainan Kokutai, the fighter was shipped via barge, along with parts from five other A6M3s found at the site, to Brisbane, in Queensland. Moved to nearby Eagle Farm in February 1943, the aircraft was returned to airworthiness by Technical Air Intelligence Unit-South West Pacific (TAIU-SWPA) personnel over subsequent months through the incorporation of missing parts obtained from the remaining abandoned Zero-sens at Buna.

The trials confirmed that due to its light weight and lower wing loading, the Zero-sen was generally more manoeuvrable than the Spitfire. While the latter enjoyed some advantages in speed, the Zero-sen had far better acceleration. The conclusion of the two test pilots that flew the aircraft was clear:

LEFT
A6M2/3 Zero-sens of the 202nd Kokutai carried X-prefixed serial numbers on the tips of their tails, as had the aircraft used by its predecessor unit, the 3rd Kokutai. Aircraft from both units were painted in standard grey-green overall, with a black engine cowling. This particular machine also had a white outline around its hinomaru, identifying that it was a Nakajima-built Zero-sen rather than one from Mitsubishi. A feature of most Zero-sen units, including the 202nd Kokutai, were command stripes – either vertical or diagonal – on the fuselage, along with horizontal stripes on the fin. These served to identify leaders and sub-leaders within the unit when in the air. IJNAF fighter pilots relied heavily on such visual aids during combat owing to the lack of functioning radio equipment in their A6M2/3s.

15

Both pilots consider the Spitfire is outclassed by the Hap [Hamp] at all heights up to 20,000ft. The Spitfire does not possess any outstanding qualifications which permits it to gain an advantage over the 'Hap' ['Hamp'] in equal circumstances.

This finding might have been a surprise for some, given that the Spitfire was a machine that had gained such a fine reputation for manoeuvrability in the European theatre. Furthermore, the trials were against the A6M3, which was less manoeuvrable than the A6M2. However, performance is relative, and the message was clear to Spitfire pilots – don't try to dogfight with a Zero-sen.

The main advantage held by the Spitfire VC over the A6M3 was its superior performance at high altitude. The combat ceiling of the IJNAF fighter was established at 32,500ft, while that of the Spitfire VC was 37,000ft. The heavier Spitfire could dive faster, so if it had the height advantage it could make diving attacks with relative impunity. The Spitfire pilot then had the choice of zooming up in preparation for another diving attack or continuing the dive and disengaging if the situation was unfavourable. However, these test results were only released *after* the 1943 air campaign over Darwin had been fought. The RAAF pilots would learn the same lessons in combat.

Other key design differences between the Spitfire VC and the A6M2/3 included the undercarriage and engine type. The Zero-sen, intended for carrier operations, had a wide undercarriage that also made it highly suitable for rough field operations. The relatively narrow track of the Spitfire undercarriage proved quite the opposite, and in northern Australia landing accidents were common until pilots got used to the conditions.

Both aircraft types were married to high performance powerplants in the Sakae and the Merlin. The latter was liquid-cooled, and this cooling system proved prone to leaks or combat damage. It also created an additional maintenance burden in an environment where engineering resources were sparse and routine mechanical procedures were often carried out in the open. The air-cooled radial Sakae engine, on the other hand, was simpler and proved a lot more rugged in service. IJNAF groundcrews were able to perform full overhauls with relatively basic facilities, and the Zero-sen developed an exceptional reputation for reliability. During operations against Darwin, several hours of over-water flying were required for each mission – usually a risky proposition for a single-engined type. However, losses were relatively uncommon and even combat-damaged machines usually managed to return to the 202nd Kokutai's main forward operating base at Penfoie airfield in Koepang, on the island of Timor.

Painted a turquoise colour, the sheet of armour plating fitted as standard behind the pilot's seat is clearly visible in this photograph of Spitfire VC EE853's restored cockpit. Crucially, the A6M2 lacked any such armoured protection for its pilot. The padding in the headrest immediately above the plating was needed to cushion the pilot's head when it jerked back after the throttle was opened and the Merlin 46's supercharger kicked in at altitude. (Author's collection)

TECHNICAL
SPECIFICATIONS

Both the Spitfire and Zero-sen were conventional monoplane fighters of similar layout. The Japanese machine had a raised canopy and cut-down rear fuselage decking which gave the pilot outstanding all-round visibility. By comparison, the Spitfire pilot's view was restricted by the raised fuselage directly behind the headrest, although this was partially offset by a bulged canopy and a rear-view mirror mounted on the windscreen framing.

Both fighters were comparable in size, although the Zero-sen had a wider wingspan, but was slightly shorter in overall length. Together with a lighter weight, this meant that the Japanese fighter had a significantly lower wing loading, and hence was more manoeuvrable. The Spitfire, however, could fly higher than the Zero-sen and was optimised for high-altitude performance. It could also achieve faster speeds in a dive, meaning that an altitude advantage was critically important if a Spitfire pilot hoped to achieve success upon entering aerial combat.

The other key difference between the two types was in respect to endurance, and in the expansive Pacific theatre a healthy range was a fundamental requirement for any mission profile. Unfortunately for the units flying the Spitfire VC in the defence of northern Australia, the fighter had a very modest range, even when using a drop tank. This duly imposed significant limitations on operations over Darwin in 1943. On the other hand, the range of the A6M2 Zero-sen was outstanding, and this had been a major factor in its unmatched success in the early part of the Pacific war.

	Spitfire VC Tropical	A6M2 Zero-sen
Powerplant	1,210hp Rolls-Royce Merlin 46 (approximately 1,400hp at altitude)	950hp Nakajima Sakae-12
Performance		
Max speed	354mph at 19,000ft	331mph 14,930ft
Service ceiling	37,000ft	32,500ft
Weights		
Empty	5,081lb	3,704lb
Loaded	7,170lb	6,164lb
Dimensions		
Span	36ft 10in.	39ft 4.7in.
Length	29ft 11in.	28ft 8in.
Height	11ft 5in.	10ft 0in.
Wing loading	28lb/ft^2	22lb/ft^2
Fuel		
Internal fuel	84 gallons	150 gallons
Drop tank	30 gallons	72 gallons
Combat radius	200 miles	600 miles

ARMAMENT

At first glance the armament of the Spitfire VC and the A6M2 Zero-sen was almost identical – both had two 20mm cannon backed up by a secondary armament of machine guns. However, the Spitfire had twice the amount of ammunition and two extra machine guns. While the 0.303-in. Browning machine guns and the 7.7mm Type 97 weapons were comparable in terms of performance, there were some important differences between the Spitfire VC's Hispano Mk II cannon and the A6M2's Type 99-1.

A 94-gallon drop tank from a Zero-sen, which was jettisoned over northern Australia prior to the fighter entering combat with No. 1 Fighter Wing Spitfires. This tank was more than twice as large as the 30-gallon drop tank used by the considerably shorter-ranged Spitfire VC. (Author's collection)

The A6M2 Zero-sen's Type 99-1s were licence-built versions of the Swiss Oerlikon FF design, which was one of the first auto-cannons to be small and light enough to be fitted in the wing of a fighter aircraft. However, this design was not ideal for air-to-air combat, owing to its relatively low muzzle velocity that made split-second deflection shots very difficult to achieve. Indeed, high-scoring IJNAF Zero-sen ace Saburo Sakai was famously quoted as saying that using the Type 99-1 cannon in aerial combat was like 'trying to hit a dragonfly with a rifle'. Nevertheless, the weapon proved rugged and reliable in service.

The firepower of the Type 99-1 cannon made the Zero-sen particularly devastating during strafing attacks against stationary aircraft. The incendiary effect of the 20mm rounds would often ignite fuel tanks in targeted aircraft – even if the tanks were empty, the residual fumes alone could cause an explosion. The manoeuvrability of the Zero-sen made it a very good gun platform for strafing, and skilled pilots could use the machine guns as 'sighters' to confirm their aim before

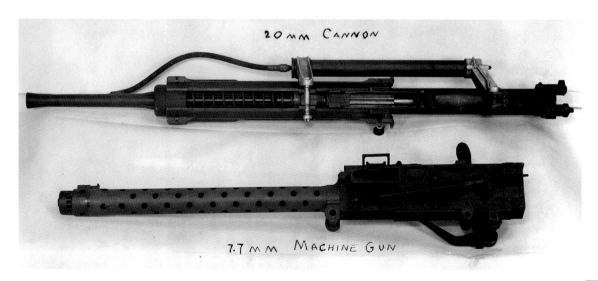

20MM CANNON

7.7MM MACHINE GUN

firing the cannon – a tactic that helped to offset the limited amount of 20mm ammunition carried.

The Spitfire VC mounted the standard British Hispano auto-cannon, which had a faster muzzle velocity and better rate of fire than the Type 99-1. It proved highly destructive against largely unarmoured Japanese aircraft that had already demonstrated their vulnerability to the much smaller US 0.50-cal machine gun round as used by the P-40E's battery of Browning M2 machine guns. However, because of the belt-fed ammunition, as well as other design issues, the Hispano as used over Darwin was a somewhat delicate weapon and was prone to failures. Furthermore, if one cannon failed, the other was almost useless as the unilateral recoil would yaw the aircraft and throw off the pilot's aim.

IN SERVICE

Since the start of the European war, Spitfires had operated from well-resourced airfields in Britain that were close to engineering support and centres of aircraft

A6M2/3 ZERO-SEN MODEL 21 ARMAMENT

The A6M2/3 was armed with two Type 99-1 20mm cannon mounted in each wing just outboard of the propeller arc, and two Type 97 7.7mm machine guns (based on the British Vickers machine gun) in the upper fuselage decking. The latter weapons, with ammunition boxes installed on either side carrying 500 rounds per gun, were synchronised to fire through the propeller. The cannon had a relatively slow maximum cyclic rate of fire of 490 rounds per minute, with each ammunition canister holding just 60 rounds per gun. In practice, this meant the Type 99-1 was a deadly weapon during strafing attacks, but it was more difficult to use for deflection shots during dogfights. In contrast to the Hispano cannon used by the Spitfire, the ammunition for the Type 99-1 was fed from a circular drum. The weapon proved both robust and reliable in service.

manufacturing. This had enabled many design changes to be introduced quickly and validated under combat conditions. However, the Spitfire VCs of No. 1 Fighter Wing would be based in a remote part of Australia, far distant from the RAAF's key technical centres, let alone those in Britain. It took the best part of a year for this support chain to become fully effective, so during 1943 the Spitfires in Darwin did not have the best technical support possible. There were numerous shortages of spare parts and even basic consumables such as drop tanks.

Technical problems also plagued the aircraft during the early months of its service introduction in Australia, with the worst of these being ineffective gun heaters. In Europe, it was found that oil in the Spitfire's guns could freeze in conditions of extreme cold. A modification was introduced whereby hot engine exhaust gases were ducted to the guns by means of aluminium piping. This was generally successful, although the 20mm Hispano cannon used in the Spitfire VC needed a heavier duty system to eradicate the problem. It was soon discovered that the aluminium piping was prone to cracking because of engine vibration, necessitating its replacement by stronger steel components.

	Spitfire VC Tropical	A6M2 Zero-sen
Primary – cannon	2 x 20mm Hispano II	2 x 20mm Type 99-1
Ammunition	belt-fed	drum
Rounds per gun	120	60
Rounds total	240	120
Secondary – machine guns	4 x 0.303-in. Brownings	2 x 7.7mm Type 97s
Rounds per gun	500	500
Rounds total	2,000	1,000

The piping change was just one is a series of technical updates driven by combat experience with the Spitfire in Britain, resulting in modification after modification. Many of these updates were issued after the fighters destined for service with No. 1 Fighter Wing had already commenced their long sea voyage to Australia, so that when they were finally assembled and flown in late 1942, they were fitted with obsolete systems – including aluminium piping. Further complicating the gun heating issue was the fact that Australian aircraft had come from different production batches, which in turn meant that they had a variety of different types of heaters fitted. Indeed, some had no gun heaters fitted at all in the belief that such equipment would not be needed in tropical conditions.

Another problem that beset the Spitfire VC related to its de Havilland-manufactured propeller and constant speed unit (CSU). At very cold temperatures at high altitudes the oil in the CSU would congeal, causing the pitch change mechanism to jam the propeller in fully fine pitch. The result was destructive over-revving of the engine to 4,000+ revolutions per minute when 3,000 was the operating limit. As No. 452 Sqn CO Sqn Ldr Ron MacDonald succinctly put it, 'You would get to around 4,200 revolutions and

SPITFIRE VC ARMAMENT

All of No. 1 Fighter Wing's Spitfire VCs were armed with two Hispano Mk II 20mm cannon and four Browning 0.303-in. machine guns. The cannon (with just 120 rounds per gun) had a useful range of 600 yards, with a total firing time of between ten and twelve seconds. They were a potentially devastating weapon, especially against unarmoured Japanese aircraft, but their belt-mounted ammunition feed proved delicate and prone to failures during aerial combat. Additionally, there were problems with obsolete gun heater mechanisms that caused armament failures at high altitude. These issues dogged the Spitfire VCs during the peak of the 1943 air campaign.

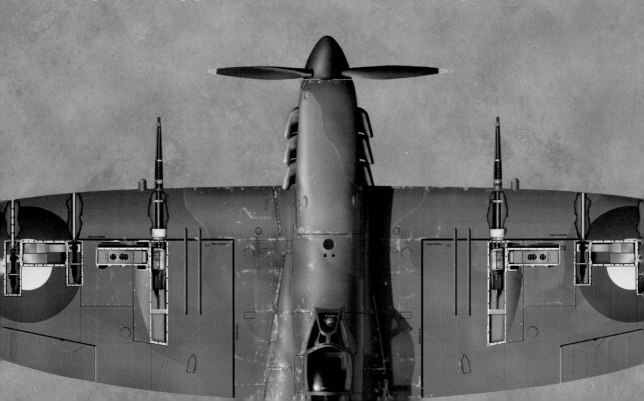

A close-up view of the engine/ propeller/spinner assembly from a crashed A6M2 recovered by the US Navy in the Aleutians in July 1942. The compact, and ultra-reliable, Nakajima Sakae-12 radial engine, with a single-stage supercharger, was rated at a modest 950hp. (NARA)

then boom!' Once this problem was identified, pilots were advised to throttle back and forth to protect the delicacy of the mechanism. However, this was never a realistic proposition for adrenaline-charged pilots going into combat at full power.

The net effect of these two problems was that at high altitude – where the Spitfire VC enjoyed a performance edge over the Zero-sen – pilots had to contend with defective guns and/or CSUs (although some of these problems occurred at lower altitudes also). Defective propellers and faulty weaponry would plague No. 1 Fighter Wing throughout the 1943 campaign.

By contrast, the Zero-sen had repeatedly shown since December 1941 that it could operate successfully from basic forward-located airfields in tropical conditions. The serviceability and reliability of the 3rd Kokutai's A6M2s during the 1942 campaign against targets in Western Australia and the Northern Territory had been excellent. This was helped by a design that had remained virtually unchanged during the preceding two years of operations leading up to 1943. Unlike the mechanical maladies that dogged the Spitfire VC, there were no niggling technical issues afflicting the Zero-sen.

By 1943 the 202nd Kokutai was augmenting its A6M2s with newly delivered A6M3s. While the latter design proved similarly robust in service, the 202nd Kokutai relied on its dependable A6M2s for Darwin operations, as these had the greater range.

During combat operations in northern Australia it was common for Spitfires to suffer numerous technical faults. If a pilot was unable to return to base and could not execute a forced landing, he would bail out if possible – the Spitfire was a dangerous aircraft to ditch at sea as it had an alarming tendency to dive underwater on impact. Fortunately, the air–sea rescue service around Darwin was very efficient, and most downed pilots could expect a speedy recovery.

STRATEGIC SITUATION

At the beginning of the 1942 dry season (typically May to October), it remained a possibility that the Japanese might try and occupy northern Australia. Accordingly, the P-40E Warhawks of the 49th FG were rushed to Darwin in the first major fighter deployment since the fall of Java. For several months the 49th FG battled Takao Kokutai G4M 'Betty' bombers escorted by 3rd Kokutai A6M3 Zero-sens, which were the principal IJNAF units ranged against Darwin at this time. However, the main axis of fighting in the Southwest Pacific quickly proved to be in New Guinea and the nearby Solomon Islands. As a result, the northern Australian air campaigns of 1942–43 involved both sides keeping a watching brief on the other while engaging in limited offensive operations.

The Japanese were concerned that Darwin might be used as a base for an Allied offensive against the NEI. However, the devastating IJN carrier raid against Darwin on 19 February 1942 had destroyed its port facilities, and as the harbour remained vulnerable to air attack, they had not been properly rebuilt. Instead, Darwin was supplied by small ships operating a shuttle from Queensland and by an overland route via the north–south Stuart Highway. While such supply routes were difficult for the Japanese to interdict with air power, they could never provide the large amount of logistics required to launch an offensive into the NEI.

Like Darwin Harbour, the RAAF base in the town had been hit hard during the 19 February attack. However, in the weeks following this raid and smaller scale follow-up attacks, significant Allied engineering resources (principally the US Army's 808th Engineer Aviation Battalion) had arrived in the Northern Territory, and they proceeded to establish a series of airfields alongside the Stuart Highway. These had

extensive and well camouflaged dispersal areas that were extremely difficult for Japanese aircraft to spot, let alone attack. Indeed, in 1943 not a single Spitfire would be lost on the ground due to enemy action – in great contrast to the many Allied fighters destroyed on Malayan and Philippine airfields during the first weeks of the war.

By 1943 two fighter strips had been completed at the '27-mile' and '34-mile' markers along the Stuart Highway, named Strauss and Livingstone, respectively. Capt Allison W. Strauss and 1Lt John Livingstone, both from the 49th FG, had been killed in action flying P-40Es during the defence of Darwin in April of the previous year. The original Darwin airfield also continued to be used by fighters, with facilities and lodgings now well dispersed some distance from the runways. Other strips along the Stuart Highway were used by the RAAF's Nos. 2 and 13 Sqns (Hudsons) and No. 31 Sqn (Beaufighters), as well as No. 18 (Dutch) Sqn (B-25 Mitchells). All of these squadrons could range into the southern fringes of the NEI, where they sometimes encountered Zero-sens from the 202nd Kokutai.

Takao Kokutai G4M1 'Bettys' en route to Darwin in 1942. This same unit would continue the bombing campaign on northern Australia the following year after being redesignated the 753rd Kokutai. A low-grade primer was used by Mitsubishi when preparing its G4Ms for painting at the factory prior to delivery to the IJNAF, and this in turn caused the green element of the bombers' camouflage scheme to readily wear off in the hot, tropical conditions encountered in the NEI. (Bob Alford)

This aerial photograph of Darwin was taken in March 1942 by a C5M 'Babs' long-range reconnaissance aircraft of the 3rd Kokutai. RAAF Base Darwin can be clearly seen in the bottom left corner of the photograph. By then it had already been largely destroyed during the raid on 19 February 1942. When No. 54 Sqn was located there in 1943, the base infrastructure had been dispersed into surrounding bushland. (AWM)

BORNEO

DUTCH
NEW GUINEA

QUEENSLAND

Gulf of Carpentaria

Babo

NORTHERN TERRITORY

Langgoer

Arafura Sea

Milingimbi

Tual

Ceram

Melville Is.

Batchelor

Darwin

Ambon

Banda Sea

Buru

Bathurst Is.

Timor Sea

Wetar

Lautem

PORT
TIMOR

WESTERN AUSTRALIA

Drysdale

N E T H E R L A N D S   E A S T   I N D I E S

DUTCH
TIMOR

Koepang

Kendari

Roti Is.

Pare Pare

Pomelaa

Semau Is.

Derby

Celebes

Broome

Makassar

Flores Sea

Flores

INDIAN OCEAN

Surabaya

Bali

Java

N

200 miles

The USAAF's 319th Bombardment Squadron had flown from Hawaii to Iron Range airfield, in northern Queensland, in November 1942 and had commenced offensive operations against Japanese targets in New Guinea with its B-24 Liberators shortly thereafter. In early 1943, the squadron transferred to Fenton, which was one of the newly constructed airfields to the south of Darwin. From this location, the four-engined heavy bombers could fly deep into enemy territory, and they duly attacked Japanese bases at Kendari and Ambon in the NEI. Finally, the RAAF's No. 12 Sqn was also present just south of Darwin, although its Vengeance dive-bombers lacked the range to reach the NEI.

The key to any successful fighter defence of Darwin was an effective radar network, as sufficient warning was needed to allow fighters to climb to the high altitudes frequented by Japanese bombers. A network of 12 radar stations was developed, operated by the RAAF's newly formed (in December 1942) No. 44 (Radar) Wing. The most important site was at Cape Fourcroy on Bathurst Island, some 70 miles northwest of Darwin. This site gave radar coverage over the Timor Sea towards the northwest, which was the typical approach track taken by Japanese aircraft.

The Japanese had modified their tactics during the course of 1942 after the defending P-40Es of the 49th FG had downed nine 'Betty' bombers during March and April. Subsequently, the Zero-sen escorts were stepped up ahead of the bombers, thus preventing the Warhawk pilots from intercepting the 'Bettys'. The attackers also flew at higher altitudes, where the performance of the P-40E was diminished. These tactics proved successful in protecting the bombers – not a single 'Betty' was lost to the 49th FG for the remainder of that year.

By September 1942 the 49th FG had been transferred to New Guinea. Replacing it in the defence of Darwin were two RAAF fighter squadrons, Nos. 76 and 77, also equipped with P-40Es. With the onset of the wet season (November to April), Japanese operations were now much diminished. However, the CO of No. 77 Sqn, Sqn Ldr Dick Cresswell, succeeded in shooting down a 'Betty' during a night mission on

Some 21 A6M2s (split into shotais of three – the IJNAF's basic fighter formation) from the 3rd Kokutai, led by hikotaicho Lt Takahide Aioi, head for Kendari, in the NEI, in 1942. Built for the KNIL-ML in 1939–40 and captured by Japanese forces in January 1942, Kendari was the main base for the Zero-sens and 'Bettys' that targeted northern Australia in 1942–43. It was largely immune from Allied air attack until USAAF B-24 Liberators began operating from Fenton in 1943. (Bob Alford)

22 November 1942. Nevertheless, No. 1 Fighter Wing was now training at RAAF Base Richmond, 30 miles northwest of central Sydney, in preparation for its move to Darwin in 1943. The fast-climbing Spitfires with their impressive high-altitude performance seemed to offer great prospects for aerial victory during the 1943 dry season.

During September 1942 the 3rd Kokutai had sent a detachment of 21 Zero-sens and four C5M 'Babs' reconnaissance aircraft to Rabaul in support of the rapidly escalating Guadalcanal campaign, with the Takao Kokutai also despatching 20 of its 'Betty' bombers. This amounted to more than half of the IJNAF's air strength previously committed to attacks on northern Australia. When the personnel returned to their base at Kendari in early November (by which time the A6M pilots involved had claimed 48 aerial victories and 20 probables), the 3rd Kokutai had been redesignated the 202nd Kokutai and the Takao Kokutai was now the 753rd Kokutai.

While the 753rd's 'Bettys' were able to fly directly back to Kendari from Rabaul, the same could not be said for the 202nd's Zero-sens and 'Babs', which required sea transport that was not readily available. This meant that by 12 December 1942 only 22 fighters were available at Kendari for service with the unit, of which five were new, shorter-ranged, A6M3 'Hamps' that were unable to reach northern Australia. Additional Zero-sens were subsequently delivered to the 202nd in small batches, the most significant of which was ten Nakajima-built A6M2s in

A busy scene at Koepang, Timor, in 1942. Multiple Zero-sens of the 3rd Kokutai are being made ready for a mission over northern Australia while a G4M 'Betty' from the Takao Kokutai flies overhead and three more A6M2s return to base after completing a patrol. The 'X-' prefixed tail codes applied to the Zero-sens have been erased by the censor. (Bernard Baeza via Bob Alford)

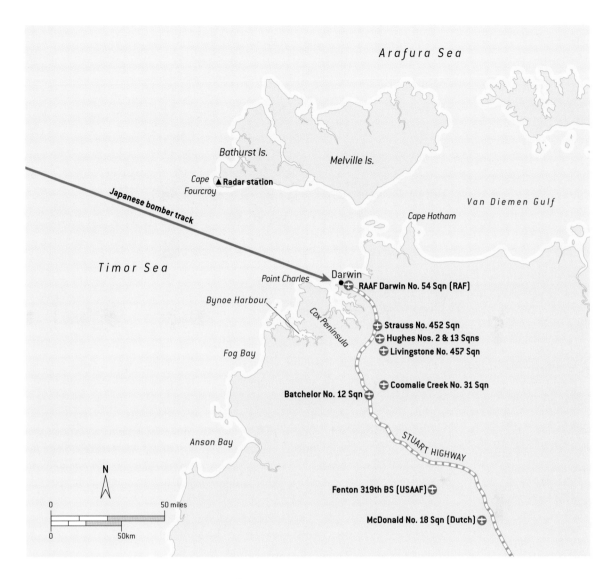

Arafura Sea

Bathurst Is.

Melville Is.

Cape Fourcroy ▲ **Radar station**

Japanese bomber track

Van Diemen Gulf

Cape Hotham

Timor Sea

Point Charles **Darwin**
⊕ **RAAF Darwin No. 54 Sqn (RAF)**

Bynoe Harbour

Cox Peninsula

⊕ **Strauss No. 452 Sqn**
⊕ **Hughes Nos. 2 & 13 Sqns**
⊕ **Livingstone No. 457 Sqn**

Fog Bay

⊕ **Coomalie Creek No. 31 Sqn**

Batchelor No. 12 Sqn ⊕

Anson Bay

STUART HIGHWAY

N

0 _____ 50 miles
0 _____ 50km

Fenton 319th BS (USAAF) ⊕

McDonald No. 18 Sqn (Dutch) ⊕

February 1943. By July of that year overall numbers had been largely restored, with 63 Zero-sens on strength at Kendari. However, attrition exacted a heavy toll on the kokutai, with only 37 of the fighters being fit for operations at that time. Indeed, by then the establishment strength of the 202nd Kokutai had been reduced to 48 aircraft (36 operational and 12 spares). This was a force strength reduction of a quarter compared to fighter numbers for much of 1942, when the 3rd Kokutai had typically fielded 45 operational A6M2s, with a further 15 spares.

The 202nd's primary airfield at Kendari was relatively safe from Allied air attacks until 1943. The unit's main forward operating base was at Koepang, from where the Zero-sens could reach Darwin. However, Koepang was in turn within range of the 20mm cannon-armed Beaufighters of No. 31 Sqn, and the IJNAF had to be wary of the vulnerability of their aircraft when using the base. Indeed, the twin-engined Beaufighters proved to be as deadly as the Zero-sens when it came to strafing parked aircraft.

A Darwin area map showing the key airfields located along the Stuart Highway to the south of Darwin. Strauss, Livingstone and Darwin itself were used by No. 1 Fighter Wing in 1943. By this time there were also several radar stations – operated by the RAAF's No. 44 (Radar) Wing – around Darwin, with the site at Cape Fourcroy, on Bathurst Island, being the most important when it came to giving the wing advanced warning of incoming raids.

Aside from the Darwin operations, the 202nd Kokutai also had defensive duties to perform over a wide area of the eastern part of the NEI. Aside from Kendari and Koepang, the unit also flew from Makassar, Ambon and Surabaya, Babo in Dutch New Guinea, Langgoer in the Kai Islands and Tual in the Tanimbar Islands.

Two No. 54 Sqn Spitfire VCs sit at readiness between missions at one of the bush airstrips built along the Stuart Highway to the south of Darwin. The bushland canopy was retained close to the runway to ensure the adjoining dispersal bays were well camouflaged from Japanese reconnaissance aircraft. This measure proved to be successful, for no Spitfires were lost on the ground as a result of the Japanese raids. However, it meant a narrow landing area that initially resulted in a high accident rate. Flying BS305/DL-J (at right) on 15 March 1943, Flg Off Granville 'Al' Mawer shot a Zero-sen down into Darwin harbour. (Andrew Thomas Collection)

The parent unit of both the 202nd and 753rd Kokutais was the 23rd Koku-sentai (Air Flotilla), and in late 1942 an order was received which recognised that the reduction in aircraft strength would be ongoing into 1943. According to order No. 127 of the Navy Staff Section, raids against Darwin would take place 'more than once a month' in the knowledge that 'available air strength in the Southwestern Area [would] gradually decrease with the progress of the situation of air combat in the Southeastern Area'. This order for raids at least once per month was consistent with maintaining a threat against Darwin that would both cause the Allies to station defensive forces there and hopefully prevent offensive forces from assembling in northern Australia in preparation for attacks on the NEI. To guard against the latter, another key mission was that of reconnaissance. This had been undertaken by 3rd Kokutai C5M 'Babs' in 1942, with these vulnerable aircraft often flying with an escort of Zero-sens.

In October 1942, the IJAAF's 70th Dokuritsu Hiko Chutai (Direct Command Squadron (DCS)) arrived in Timor equipped with the Ki-46-II 'Dinah' twin-engined reconnaissance aircraft. These sleek Mitsubishi machines were both fast and high-flying, and they began undertaking photo-reconnaissance operations over northern Australia from December using a newly constructed Timorese airfield at Lautem. The IJAAF was confident that the 'Dinah' could operate over northern Australia with impunity, as its impressive speed (375mph at 20,000ft) and ability to climb to 35,200ft made the aircraft impossible for the P-40Es to intercept.

From December 1942 to February 1943, the 202nd Kokutai prepared for the upcoming dry season campaign. Many lessons had been learned over Guadalcanal that were drilled into the newer pilots by the veterans. Indeed, the Zero-sen pilots had become used to extraordinarily long-range missions, as the distance from Rabaul to Guadalcanal was 600 miles. Accordingly, the 202nd Kokutai pilots concentrated on 'over-ocean navigation techniques' and 'formation fighting tactics'.

The scene was set for the 1943 campaign. The 'Dinahs' of the 70th DCS would monitor northern Australia and identify targets for raids by 753rd Kokutai 'Betty' bombers escorted by 202nd Kokutai Zero-sens. They would in turn be opposed by the three Spitfire VC squadrons of No. 1 Fighter Wing.

THE COMBATANTS

No. 1 FIGHTER WING

The origins of No. 1 Fighter Wing are interesting, as the RAAF had no modern fighters of its own at the start of World War II. It was assumed that Great Britain would guarantee Australia's security via the basing of a battle fleet in Singapore. In return, the RAAF would focus on training aircrew for use by the RAF as part of a plan known in Australia as the Empire Air Training Scheme (EATS). The threat to Australia, in the context of a global war against Germany, would be limited to 'cruiser raids', and the need for air defence was therefore remote. Accordingly, for home defence the RAAF focused on seawards reconnaissance, raising several squadrons equipped with Hudson light bombers and Catalina flying boats.

During 1940–41 the RAAF underwent rapid expansion, but this was mostly in the context of EATS, which intended to provide almost 10,000 trained airmen annually. Some of the Australian EATS pilots would eventually serve in RAF fighter squadrons, including in four 'Australian' fighter squadrons as provided by Article XV of the EATS agreement. Other Australian pilots gained fighter experience while serving with No. 3 Sqn (RAAF) in North Africa, which initially flew Gladiator biplanes. Similarly, No. 21 Sqn (RAAF) was sent to Malaya, where it was equipped with Buffalo fighters.

After the Pacific War started, following the surprise attack on the US Navy's Pacific Fleet base at Pearl Harbor on 7 December 1941, Australian territory came under enemy occupation when Rabaul, in New Guinea, fell to the Japanese in January 1942. In the following month Australia experienced a double shock when 'Fortress Singapore' surrendered on 15 February and Darwin was attacked by more than 200 IJNAF aircraft four days later. The Australian government's defence plans were now in

disarray, but fortunately shipments of USAAC P-40E Warhawk and P-39 Airacobra fighters were already arriving in Australia. A sufficient number of P-40Es were transferred to the RAAF on an emergency basis to enable the formation of Nos. 75, 76 and 77 Sqns.

At this time the Australian government began lobbying both London and Washington for a sufficient allocation of modern aircraft to enable an urgent expansion of the RAAF. To this end the Australian Minister for External Affairs, Dr H. V. Evatt, travelled to London to appeal directly to British Prime Minister Winston Churchill. As a result of their meeting on 28 May 1942, Churchill agreed to send three Spitfire squadrons to Australia. So it was that the so-called 'Churchill Wing' was entirely a political invention, playing on the close ties between Australia and Britain. While far-dwarfed by the American resources allocated to the defence of the Southwest Pacific, the symbolism of the 'Churchill Wing' was highly significant, and a boost for British prestige that had suffered after the fall of Singapore.

The political weight behind this decision ensured the quick despatch of aircraft to Australia, and very soon 42 Spitfires were at sea bound for Melbourne. However, on 21 June 1942, the besieged Libyan port town of Tobruk was captured by Axis forces and the unfolding emergency led to the Spitfires being unloaded in West Africa, from where they would be flown to Egypt. The subsequent delay in allocating replacements meant the first six Spitfires did not arrive in Australia until August. However, by the end of 1942 more than 100 had been received – enough to equip the new wing fully and provide for a pool of reserves. Shipments continued into 1943, and by the end of that year the RAAF had received a total of 244 Spitfire VCs (plus a single VB). The new fighters were given the RAAF serial prefix A58.

Meanwhile, the new wing had been designated No. 1 Fighter Wing, and it was allocated three existing Spitfire squadrons from Britain. Two of these were obvious choices, Nos. 452 and 457 Sqns, which were two of the four Australian EATS fighter units and the only ones flying Spitfires. The third was a regular RAF unit, No. 54 Sqn, which had a distinguished history that included seeing extensive combat during the Battle of Britain. However, the move to Australia was not a popular one within the three squadrons, as Anthony Cooper described in his book *Darwin Spitfires*:

> They came unwillingly, loath to give up their comfortable bases in England and their
> high-profile role in the cross-Channel war against Hitler's 'Fortress Europe'.

There may well have been an assumption in Australia that all three squadrons were veterans of the Battle of Britain. However, the two EATS units had not formed until early 1941, and no EATS pilots had graduated early enough to see combat in the summer of 1940. While No. 54 Sqn had indeed fought in the Battle of Britain, by late 1942 virtually all of the pilots from that period had been posted elsewhere. This was in line with RAF expansion doctrine, which meant that pilots with hard-won combat experience were needed to staff training units or for middle-level administrative duties. Hence, despite No. 54 Sqn's fine pedigree, it was in fact the most inexperienced unit of the three.

By the time of the Darwin campaign, only three of No. 54 Sqn's pilots were considered combat experienced. Indeed, the unit was led by newly promoted Sqn Ldr Eric 'Bill' Gibbs who had been transferred in from Coastal Command and who had no operational fighter experience at all – nevertheless, he would subsequently acquit himself admirably in the defence of Darwin. He was assisted by two combat-experienced flight commanders in Flt Lts Bob Foster (a Battle of Britain veteran and also a future ace) and Robin Norwood.

Norwood had joined No. 54 Sqn in April 1942, which since the previous November had been at RAF Castletown in the far north of Scotland. At this time the unit was in the process of replacing its weary Spitfire IIAs with Mk VBs (it had briefly flown Mk VA/Bs when assigned to the Channel Front with No. 11 Group in 1941) and morale was poor. The squadron had endured a harsh winter and its *espirit de corps* had been lost through a seemingly endless series of postings. In one single month 22 experienced pilots had left, an entry in the unit's Operations Record Book noting at the time:

> The Squadron is becoming a kind of Operational Training Unit [OTU] – as soon as someone gets well trained, he is posted. The whole squadron is completely browned off and constantly praying that the 'powers that be' will have mercy on us and grant us a spell of duty in civilised England.

In late May 1942 the unit was told to prepare for an overseas posting. It then underwent further turmoil as non-British pilots were posted out in order to make it an exclusively British squadron. This was another political expedient, as No. 54 Sqn would become the sole RAF representative in the Pacific theatre.

How did the combat experience of the two EATS units compare with No. 54 Sqn? Neither had a long history, with No. 452 Sqn being the first Australian EATS unit to form in Britain. Declared operational in May 1941, it subsequently became one of the most successful squadrons in Fighter Command over the coming nine months. In operations over England and France, its pilot claimed 62 enemy aircraft destroyed. However, many of these victories were attributed to two outstanding aces – Irishman Brendan 'Paddy' Finucane and Australian Keith 'Bluey' Truscott, neither of whom would accompany the squadron to Australia. Indeed, No. 452 Sqn's experience mirrored that of No. 54 Sqn, as most of its pilots were posted elsewhere prior to the unit leaving Britain. Just two experienced aviators would remain during the move to Australia. One of these men was the newly appointed CO, Sqn Ldr Ray Thorold-Smith, who had achieved the necessary five victories to be awarded the Distinguished Flying Cross (DFC) in late 1941.

These three individuals were heavily involved in operations with No. 452 Sqn during 1941–42. Flt Lts Keith 'Bluey' Truscott, Brendan 'Paddy' Finucane and Ray 'Throttle' Thorold-Smith all made multiple claims while serving with the unit in Britain. The first two, both high-scoring aces, left the squadron prior to its departure for Australia, while Thorold-Smith (also an ace) took over from Truscott as No. 452 Sqn's commanding officer in March 1942. He would lead it into battle over Darwin in 1943. (AWM)

The experience of No. 457 Sqn was somewhat different. Based on the Isle of Man, it only became operational in August 1941 and effectively served as an OTU for the likes of No. 452 Sqn. Prior to embarkation for Australia in mid-1942, No. 457 saw two months' service over northern France under the command of Battle of Britain ace Sqn Ldr Pete Brothers, during which time it lost 11 aircraft and had eight pilots killed. Despite this limited experience, the squadron had been 'blooded' and arrived in Australia with a strong core cadre of pilots (but minus Brothers, who categorically refused to travel to Australia) much less diluted by postings than the other two squadrons.

The choice of who was to lead No. 1 Fighter Wing into combat was a challenging one for the RAAF, as it was under immense political pressure to achieve immediate success. A steady and competent leader might have been found among the pool of middle-ranking permanent officers, but instead the selection was made of a Wing Commander Flying who would help sate the public's need for a locally identifiable version of 'one of the few'. The man chosen for the job was Wg Cdr Clive Caldwell, who had claimed 22 victories in North Africa in 1941–42 flying Tomahawks and Kittyhawks and would remain Australia's highest scoring ace of the war.

Although Caldwell was an early EATS graduate, he had in fact joined the RAAF upon the outbreak of war, but had not wanted to become an instructor after completing his flying training. He duly resigned his commission and enrolled in an EATS course instead. In May 1941 Caldwell was posted to the Middle East, where he joined the recently formed No. 250 Sqn (RAF) equipped with Tomahawk IIBs. Over the next year Caldwell flew some 300 combat sorties totalling 550 hours, engaging German and Italian fighters and dive-bombers over the North African desert. He routinely fought Bf 109E/Fs flown by veteran Luftwaffe pilots, claiming ten of them shot down. Awarded a DFC and Bar in December 1941, Caldwell was promoted to squadron leader the following month and given command of Kittyhawk I-equipped No. 112 Sqn (RAF). This appointment made him the first EATS graduate to lead a British squadron.

There is little doubt that Caldwell was a brilliant pilot and expert marksmen. He famously advocated the practice of shooting at aircraft shadows over the desert as a training method. Also, Caldwell was the right age to lead the young pilots of No. 1 Fighter Wing, being 31 years old at the start of 1943. However, Caldwell was a rugged individualist, and his leadership would be tested in a number of ways – not least by permanent officers who perhaps resented his exceptionally rapid rise through the ranks. On the other hand, Caldwell was exactly the type of fighter pilot hero the Australian press, and local politicians, wanted. Partly for his proclivity for strafing enemy ground targets at any opportunity, the ace was universally known as 'Killer Caldwell' – a nickname he could never shake.

202nd KOKUTAI

The 202nd Kokutai was the only Zero-sen unit to engage Spitfires in the skies over Darwin in 1943. It had a remarkable combat history (rarely alluded to in Western sources) prior to the clashes with No. 1 Fighter Wing, and this helps to explain the exceptional proficiency of its pilots during the engagements of 1943. Even after significant wastage of its best leaders during the campaign in Guadalcanal in the second half of 1942, the 202nd Kokutai's standard of airmanship in 1943 was among the highest produced by any IJNAF unit during the war.

As previously mentioned in this volume, prior to a re-numbering on 1 November 1942, the 202nd Kokutai had originally been known as the 3rd Kokutai. First established as a G4M 'Betty' bomber unit on 10 April 1941, it had initially seen combat from Hanoi over China. In mid-September 1941 the 3rd Kokutai had been re-formed at Takao, on Formosa (now Taiwan), as a fighter unit with an establishment strength of 54 A6M2s and nine C5M2s.

Many of the pilots transferred into the 3rd Kokutai had come from the 12th Kokutai, which had been disbanded on 15 September 1941. It was a veteran of the Sino–Japanese War, having been established in China in July 1937 with fighters, dive-bombers and torpedo-bombers. In 1938 the 12th had become a fighter-only unit, operating A5M 'Claudes', and in July 1940 it received the first 15 A6M2 Model 11s to be issued to a frontline kokutai. These had the range to escort bombers deep into inland China, and on the fourth such mission on 13 September 1940 the Zero-sen made its combat debut. Thirteen A6M2s met some 30 RoCAF Polikarpov I-15 and I-16 fighters near Chongqing and gave them a severe mauling. The Chinese lost 13 aircraft (the IJNAF pilots lodged claims for 27) and failed to down a single Zero-sen in return. It was an auspicious start for the new fighter, and such was the outstanding performance of the Zero-sen in China that the RoCAF soon avoided aerial engagements altogether.

By forming with a strong cadre of battle-hardened 12th Kokutai pilots, the 3rd Kokutai could claim direct lineage to both the early days of the Sino–Japanese War and the combat debut of the Zero-sen. Furthermore, even the non-combat experienced pilots that transferred into the unit typically had at least 1,000 flying hours in their logbooks. Clearly, this was the most solid of foundations with which to build an elite fighter unit.

In the weeks prior to the commencement of the Pacific War the 3rd Kokutai flew myriad training missions from Takao, sharing the airfield with another newly constituted Zero-sen unit in the form of the Tainan Kokutai. One of the key tasks undertaken by the 3rd Kokutai during this period was to conduct long-range flying trials to prepare pilots for the missions they would have to perform escorting IJNAF bombers charged with hitting key US military targets on Luzon, in the Philippines – 500 miles from Takao. Techniques were developed that minimised fuel consumption to such a degree that missions of 600 miles could be flown with an allowance of 20 minutes for combat over the target. This was an extraordinary distance for a fighter to cover in 1941.

On 8 December 1941 the 3rd Kokutai undertook the first of these long-range missions that effectively neutralised USAAC air power in the Philippines. Leading the unit was hikotochio Lt Tamotsu Yokoyama, who had led the first six Zero-sens sent to China in July 1940. The 3rd Kokutai A6M2s, along with those of the accompanying Tainan Kokutai, had luck on their side. During the early hours of 8 December, American forces in the Philippines received word of the Pearl Harbor attack of the previous day and the USAAC scrambled the majority of its fighter force in full expectation of a raid from Formosa. However, heavy fog delayed the IJNAF aircraft for several hours, and they did not arrive over Luzon until after midday.

The subsequent attack could not have been better timed, with many of the American aircraft caught on the ground refuelling. During this and further missions flown on 10 December, the USAAC lost dozens of aircraft and was effectively reduced to half its pre-war strength in the Philippines. While the Zero-sen pilots from the 3rd Kokutai were credited with shooting down 21 P-35s and P-40s in aerial combat, many more American fighters, bombers and flying boats were destroyed on the ground. Overall, the Luzon missions were a stunning success for the Japanese, and the tally of USAAC and US Navy aircraft destroyed would have been appreciably less had the attacks been undertaken exclusively by bombers. Further missions continued throughout December, although with much diminished American opposition. Just five pilots from the 3rd Kokutai were lost during the Philippine operations.

On 23 December 1941 the 3rd Kokutai redeployed to Davao, in the southern Philippines, from where it could strike south against the NEI. Three days later six A6M2s flew 450 miles to Lake Tondano, in the Celebes, which was being used as a flying boat anchorage. Here, the Zero-sens destroyed four Do 24 flying boats of the *Marineluchtvaartdienst* (Royal Netherlands Naval Air Service, or MLD). The raid was an unpleasant surprise for the Dutch who had believed that the anchorage was safe from attack by land-based aircraft. On 28 December yet another audacious long-range mission was flown against the strategic oil-producing centre of Tarakan, in Borneo – a distance of 600 miles. Seven A6M2s were led to the target by a C5M, where they were met by four Buffalos of the *Militaire Luchtvaart van het Koninklijk Nederlands-Indisch Leger* (Royal Netherlands East Indies Army Air Force, or KNIL-ML). Three of the Brewster fighters were shot down, while the fourth crash-landed. In return, one of the A6M2s was moderately damaged.

The Davao deployment confirmed the 3rd Kokutai's ability to deploy long distances to newly captured airfields and then to rapidly launch missions deep into enemy territory. This was the pattern of NEI operations over the coming weeks, and it allowed the Japanese to retain the initiative and repeatedly catch Allied forces unprepared. A major factor in this success in the NEI was the capture of fully serviceable Dutch aerodromes, with their attendant supplies of fuels, lubricants and other materials all virtually intact.

On 11 January 1942 the invasion of Menado, in the Celebes, commenced, with this operation being largely covered by Zero-sens from the 3rd Kokutai. These aircraft shot down four of the five RAAF Hudsons that attempted to attack the invading troops. Following the capture of Menado, the 3rd Kokutai immediately commenced moving 35 A6M2s there. On 15 January, 18 Zero-sens headed from Menado to Ambon Island (a distance of 425 miles), where they encountered just two KNIL-ML Buffalos – the island's sole fighter defence. Both aircraft were quickly downed by the attackers.

Capt Gaifu Kamei (left) and Lt Cdr Takeo Shibata (centre), respectively the commanding officer and executive officer of the 3rd Kokutai, watch Zero-sens take-off from Takao on 8 December 1941, bound for Luzon. The unit was led aloft by hikotaicho Lt Tamotsu Yokoyama. The identity of the third officer on the platform is unknown. (Tony Holmes Collection)

A major positive for the IJNAF Zero-sen pilots was the capture of Kendari, in the Celebes, following an amphibious assault on the night of 23–24 January. The town boasted a very large, centrally located, airfield that was in fact one of the best in the whole of the NEI. Only completed in 1940, it featured paved all-weather runways – although Kendari's fickle weather patterns sometimes restricted flying. The 3rd Kokutai moved into Kendari on 25 January, and once again the unit's ability to launch operations quickly was impressive, for the very next day two missions were generated.

In the first of these, six A6M2s attacked Koepang, where two Dutch airliners were destroyed on the ground and an RAAF DC-2 was forced to ditch into the sea. The second mission saw three Zero-sens attack Namlea and Ambon, where they destroyed several RAAF Hudsons on the ground. However, on this occasion, the 3rd Kokutai suffered its first fatalities since mid-December when one pilot was killed in action and another was lost while attempting a forced-landing during the return flight to Kendari.

On 2 February, the 3rd Kokutai deployed to Balikpapan, on the island of Borneo, from where it could fly missions over eastern Java. The next day 27 A6M2s took off to cover two bomber formations targeting Surabaya naval base and Madiun – another long-range mission of more than 500 miles. The Zero-sens ran into 19 KNIL-ML fighters (CW-21Bs and Hawk 75As). In the swirling dogfight that ensued, more than a dozen of the Dutch fighters were downed or were damaged and forced to crash-land. In return, three Zero-sens were shot down. On 5 February, two formations of fighters from the 3rd Kokutai were despatched to attack Denpasar (on Bali) and Surabaya. The latter group accounted for two KNIL-ML Hawk 75As and an MLD Catalina shot down. Over Bali, the Denpasar formation encountered ten USAAC P-40Es that had just taken off after refuelling. Five of the Warhawks were shot down without loss to the 3rd Kokutai.

The 3rd Kokutai suffered another fatality on 9 February when FPO1c Masayuki Nakase was shot down while strafing Dutch armoured cars in Makassar. Killed in the subsequent crash of his A6M2, Nakase had flown Zero-sens with the 12th Kokutai in China in 1940. He had also been one of the 3rd Kokutai's leading aces, with a personal score of 18 victories by the time of his death.

Flying from the newly captured airfield at Makassar on 20 February, several 3rd Kokutai Zero-sens were patrolling the waters around Bali – Japanese ships had just landed troops on the island – when they spotted seven USAAC A-24 dive-bombers and their escort of 16 P-40Es. In the hard-fought engagement that ensued, two of the Warhawks were shot down and Sea1c Tomekichi Otsuki was killed.

By then only Java remained in Allied hands, and Zero-sens from both the 3rd and Tainan Kokutais were routinely operating over the island as Allied defences crumbled. On 27 February, 15 A6M2s from the 3rd Kokutai escorted 'Betty' bombers targeting the aircraft carrier USS *Langley* (CV-1), which was attempting to transport 32 crated P-40Es to the Javanese port of Tjiltjap for the USAAC's 13th Pursuit Squadron (Provisional). In the absence of aerial opposition, the Zero-sen pilots took the opportunity to strafe the flight deck of the US Navy's first carrier, which was later finished off by its escorting destroyers after the vessel was left dead in the water following the attack by the 'Betty' bombers. That same day an Allied naval force was soundly defeated by the IJN during the Battle of the Java Sea, allowing the invasion of Java to begin on 1 March. After a week of fighting, the Dutch surrendered on the 8th.

During February, Allied aircraft had pioneered a new air route between Java and the town of Broome, on the remote northwest Australian coast. By the time Java was invaded, evacuation flights were underway in earnest. Among the many aircraft arriving in Broome were USAAC B-17E and LB-30 heavy bombers, MLD flying boats and Dutch airliners. The Japanese confirmed this activity when a 3rd Kokutai C5M overflew Broome on 2 March. The unit organised a strike against the distant target the very next day, with the pilots having to fly more than 600 miles from

The remains of a USAAC B-24A Liberator that was strafed and destroyed at Broome during the highly successful raid mounted by nine A6M2s from the 3rd Kokutai on 3 March 1942. (Russ Rayson via David Vincent)

Koepang to Broome. Virtually the entire route was over open ocean, without the benefit of any navigational landmarks. Nevertheless, Japanese airmanship was faultless, with a lone C5M leading nine Zero-sens to Broome, where they arrived overhead at 0930 hrs. They found a target-rich environment, as many aircraft had flown in that morning and were waiting to be refuelled.

Once again, the A6M2s proved to be deadly in their strafing role. Anchored in the natural harbour at Broome were 15 flying boats, while there were six large aircraft at the nearby airfield. All were destroyed. A lone B-24A that had just taken off was also despatched, although a gunner onboard the bomber was possibly responsible for shooting down its attacker, FPO1c Osamu Kudo, who was killed. On the return flight, the Zero-sens intercepted and forced down a Dutch DC-3 – a second A6M2 ran out of fuel shortly afterwards and was ditched, its pilot being rescued by the IJN. All told, the Allies lost 23 valuable multi-engined aircraft, and at least 86 people were killed.

With the surrender of Java five days after the Broome attack, the Japanese conquest of Southeast Asia was complete. It is difficult to quantify exactly how many aircraft the 3rd Kokutai had destroyed between 8 December 1941 and 8 March 1942, with pilots from the unit claiming 150 aerial victories and 50 strafing kills. In return, 14 pilots from the 3rd Kokutai are known to have been killed and perhaps as many as 20 A6M2s lost.

AUSTRALIA – 1942 DRY SEASON CAMPAIGN

Following the fall of Java, the key target for the 3rd Kokutai's continuing offensive operations was Darwin. The port and airfield there had already been decimated by the raids on 19 February by both carrier-based aircraft and land-based bombers. Despite Darwin being 500 miles from the 3rd Kokutai's Koepang airfield, it became a regular mission for the unit's Zero-sen pilots during 1942.

On 16 March, six A6M2s escorted fourteen Takao Kokutai 'Bettys' that attacked RAAF Base Darwin, this mission establishing the pattern for regular raids in coming months. The Takao Kokutai had originally formed at Takao airfield on Formosa, and it was later redesignated the 753rd Kokutai. It would rely exclusively on Zero-sens from the 3rd/202nd Kokutai for protection over Darwin in 1942–43.

Their cockpits shrouded from the boiling sunshine by cleverly rigged tarpaulins, a pair of A6M2s from the 3rd Kokutai sit quietly between missions at Lakunai airfield, Rabaul, in September 1942. More than half the unit's strength (27 pilots and their aircraft) were transported to Rabaul on board the carrier *Taiyo*. During a two-month period of fighting over Guadalcanal, in the Solomon Islands, the 3rd Kokutai lost eight aircraft and six pilots in combat. Parked behind the fighters is an L3Y 'Tina' transport aircraft, developed from the G3M 'Nell' bomber. (Tony Holmes Collection)

A group portrait of the pilots and groundcrew sent by the 3rd Kokutai to Lakunai in September 1942. A total of 21 Zero-sens and four 'Babs' were shipped to Rabaul under the command of Lt Cdr Kiyoji Sakakibara, who is seen here in the second row, sat eighth from left. To his left is the kokutai's hikotaicho, and ten-victory ace, Lt Takahide Aioi, who would subsequently lead the (redesignated) 202nd Kokutai over Darwin in early 1943. (Tony Holmes Collection)

On the Allied side, there was one benefit from the loss of the NEI – no more fighters would be rushed there. To this end, three P-40E squadrons from the USAAF's 49th FG were assigned to the defence of Darwin, with the first aircraft arriving in mid-March. Darwin's first radar station also became operational at this time (22 March).

The 3rd Kokutai first clashed with the 49th FG on 30 and 31 March. Despite a number of claims by both sides, just one P-40E was shot down, while the Japanese suffered no Zero-sen losses (although one 'Betty' was destroyed). The activity continued into April, with five daylight raids being made on Darwin by 'Bettys' flying at around 20,000ft. For the first time the Zero-sen escorts (usually only single chutais of nine aircraft) were met by large numbers of P-40Es, with as many as 50 at a time being sent aloft. In fighter-versus-fighter combat, just one Zero-sen was lost in exchange for six P-40Es. However, some of the American pilots were able to get through to the bombers, downing eight 'Bettys' during the course of the month.

May, by contrast, was quiet, as the Takao Kokutai rebuilt its losses and elements of the 3rd Kokutai deployed to Rabaul to support operations there that culminated in the Battle of the Coral Sea, fought during 4–8 May. While just single chutais of Zero-sens had escorted most of the April missions, when the raids recommenced the 3rd Kokutai bolstered its support of the bombers by despatching formations of between 21 and 45 A6M2s for the four raids mounted in June. A series of largescale aerial engagements duly ensued, and this time the 3rd Kokutai was successful in defending the bombers, as none were lost. The unit again had the upper hand in the skies over Darwin, losing two Zero-sens in exchange for nine P-40Es destroyed.

July saw the Takao Kokutai 'Bettys' make several night raids on Darwin, followed by just one daylight mission on the 30th. On this day 27 Zero-sens fought 36 P-40Es, with a single fighter from both sides being lost. The next daylight raid, on 13 August, saw 27 Zero-sens intercepted by 24 P-40Es, and it resulted in the 3rd Kokutai suffering its worst losses over Darwin when four A6M2s were shot down. While 'Bettys' continued to fly night raids up until 25 November, the 3rd Kokutai saw no

Post-war historians have criticised No. 1 Fighter Wing for employing obsolete line astern formation tactics in 1943 during the defence of northern Australia. Aircraft would operate in pairs, and in theory one pair would cover another pair of fighters. However, the trailing wingmen could not be covered by their leaders, and in every formation there would always be a weaving 'tail-end Charlie' who was liable to be picked off by the enemy. These failures were exacerbated by a tendency for formations to break up quickly into individual actions during combat, although towards the end of the campaign the tactics being employed by the wing were much improved as a result of growing combat experience.

A6M2s of the 3rd Kokutai soon after arriving in the NEI in early 1942. Using tactics that fully exploited the Zero-sen's unrivalled long-range, this unit enjoyed enormous success against Allied air units in the Philippines and the NEI during the first few months of the war. (Bob Alford)

further combat over Darwin for the rest of the year following its poor showing on 13 August.

During 1942, a total of eight Zero-sens had been lost in combat over Darwin and eight pilots killed. In return, 17 P-40Es were shot down, although that must be balanced against the loss of nine 'Bettys'. Of the four pilots killed on the 3rd Kokutai's black day on 13 August, two had only just graduated from flight school earlier that same year. Their demise indicated that growing combat losses were now having an impact on the unit, and it could no longer rely on all of its pilots being experienced 1,000-hour veterans.

The struggle for Guadalcanal had begun in August, and detachments from both the Takao and 3rd Kokutais were sent to support the bloody campaign in September. More than half the strength of the 3rd Kokutai (27 pilots and their aircraft) were transported to Rabaul on board the carrier *Taiyo*. During a two-month period in the Solomon Islands, the 3rd Kokutai lost eight aircraft and six pilots in combat.

PREPARATION FOR BATTLE

Just after Prime Minister Winston Churchill agreed to send three Spitfire squadrons to Australia, Sqn Ldr Clive Caldwell arrived in Britain in June 1942 and was posted as a supernumerary wing leader to the Kenley Wing, located a short distance south of London in Surrey. Here, he gained experience with Spitfire VBs and flew a series of sorties over northern France, where he tangled with both Bf 109s and Fw 190s. More significantly, he gained experience leading the wing and in 'Balbo' tactics.

'Balbo' or 'Big Wing' tactics involved trying to intercept enemy formations with an entire wing of three 12-aircraft squadrons. This would hopefully ensure numerical superiority when the engagement commenced, and thus increase the chances of a decisive victory. However, the process of forming up the entire wing took time and burnt fuel, which the short-ranged Spitfire could ill afford to lose. Caldwell's adoption of 'Balbo' tactics would be controversial over Darwin.

The ace arrived back in Australia in September. The following month he reported to No. 2 OTU at Mildura, in northwestern Victoria, which was the RAAF's sole fighter training unit. Here, Caldwell mixed with local pilots and learnt about Japanese aircraft and their capabilities. At the end of November, he was posted to the newly formed No. 1 Fighter Wing. Caldwell's role was that of the airborne leader of the wing, and his rank at this time was acting Wing Commander (from 1 January 1943). A permanent RAAF officer, 37-year-old Gp Capt Allan 'Wally' Walters, was actually in command.

No. 1 Fighter Wing was formally raised on 7 October 1942 at RAAF Base Richmond, northwest of Sydney, where the three squadrons had arrived after the lengthy sea journey from Britain. Caldwell found a somewhat restless group of pilots,

A group of No. 1 Fighter Wing pilots soon after arriving in Australia in late 1942. Most are sporting summer uniforms. Flt Lt Robin Norwood is second from right, while Battle of Britain veteran Flt Lt Bob Foster is standing in the front row second from left. The tall pilot in the back row is Sqn Ldr Ray 'Throttle' Thorold-Smith. (Ralph Murphy)

The standard Japanese fighter element was a shotai of three aircraft flying in an echeloned V. By European standards, this was an obsolete formation ('finger four' or line abreast had been adopted by the Luftwaffe following lessons learned in the Spanish Civil War, while the RAF was slowly switching from line astern to a similar formation by 1943), but the IJNAF made it highly functional by virtue of the exceptional teamwork and keen situational awareness of the Japanese fighter pilots. On the rare occasion where a Spitfire was briefly on the tail of a Zero-sen in 1943, the usual outcome was for the No. 1 Fighter Wing pilot to be quickly fired on by one or both of the remaining A6M2/3s from the shotai.

a number of whom had not flown operationally for an entire year. Their mindset was not helped by delays with the delivery of the Spitfires – initially only six were available. It was not until the final weeks of the year that large-scale training was possible for the entire wing.

While No. 1 Fighter Wing had no Battle of Britain aces available to it (although Flt Lt Bob Foster had seen considerable combat during that momentous summer), the other campaign most relevant to the tactical situation over Darwin was Malta. Here

The pilot of this Spitfire VC has been quick to retract the fighter's undercarriage at tree-top height moments after take-off. Following a few months of near-constant practice, No. 1 Fighter Wing's scrambles became highly efficient. (Ralph Murphy)

ROBIN NORWOOD

Born in 1910, Robin Norwood commenced his flying career in 1938 with the RAF Volunteer Reserve. He completed his intermediate and advanced training at No. 8 Flying Training School in Montrose, Angus (Scotland), with No. 19 Course, which ran from 6 May to 16 August 1940. Norwood was then posted to No. 5 OTU at Aston Down, Gloucestershire, before moving to No. 7 OTU at Hawarden, Flintshire (Wales), two days later for conversion onto the Spitfire. After accruing just 20 hours of flying in the fighter, he joined No. 65 Sqn at Turnhouse, in Edinburgh, on 2 September. This unit had been very active during the Battle of France, the evacuation of Dunkirk and in the early stages of the Battle of Britain, but fortunately for the inexperienced Norwood, the squadron had been sent to Scotland to rest six days before he joined it.

By December 1940 No. 65 Sqn had returned south to Tangmere, on the Sussex coast. However, by this time the Battle of Britain had ended and the onset of winter restricted flying. In early 1941 Norwood flew fighter sweeps over France before the squadron moved north to Kirton-in-Lindsey, in Lincolnshire. Various operational patrols were flown from here, including at night, but there were fleeting opportunities to meet the enemy. In August 1941 Norwood was posted to No. 57 OTU at Hawarden, by which time he had accrued more than 600 flying hours, and at the age of 31 was considered to be an 'old hand'. The following April, Norwood joined No. 54 Sqn at Castletown, Caithness, in northern Scotland, the unit having seen a heavy turnover of pilots. He moved with it to Australia, and was probably the most experienced Spitfire pilot in the newly formed No. 1 Fighter Wing.

Appointed a flight leader, Flt Lt Norwood was one of No. 54 Sqn's most senior pilots during the 1943 Darwin campaign. He participated in several of the large aerial battles that year and narrowly failed to shoot down a 'Dinah' on 23 May. His diary entry two days later shows the stress of continually waiting for enemy raids:

'All of us thought there would be a big raid today but it didn't happen, thank heavens. In some ways it would be better to get it over with as there is an awful tension about and it gives me nightmares. My nerves are doubtless not as good as they were and I am smoking too much.'

In 1944 Norwood undertook a brief stint at No. 2 OTU at Mildura before being assigned duty as an air ferrying pilot. Frustrated at not receiving another combat posting, he returned to Britain in 1945 and took up farming. Robin Norwood was killed in a car accident on 2 April 1970.

Flt Lt Robin Norwood joined No. 54 Sqn in Scotland in April 1942. At the start of the 1943 dry season campaign, he was the unit's most experienced Spitfire pilot. (Ralph Murphy)

Two No. 54 Sqn pilots discuss a cockpit-related issue with an airman whose hand can be seen gripping the rear-view mirror. The robin's nest artwork on the cockpit door identifies this aircraft as the Spitfire VC assigned to flight leader Flt Lt Norwood. (AWM)

TAKAHIDE AIOI

Born in Hiroshima Prefecture in 1912, Aioi graduated from the Naval Academy in 1931 as a member of the 59th class, before completing the 25th Aviation Cadet course in July 1934. He subsequently flew biplane fighters with the Tateyama Kokutai, from the light carrier *Ryujo* and with the Saeki Kokutai until the latter unit became the 12th Kokutai in July 1937. Aioi was posted with this unit to Zhoushuizi, in China's Liaoning Province, shortly thereafter following the commencement of the Second Sino–Japanese War. By September, heavy fighting had broken out around Shanghai, and the 12th Kokutai deployed its Type 95 biplane fighters to nearby Kunda airfield. From here, Aioi flew patrols over the frontline in support of IJN ground troops. By the end of the year, he had been promoted to lieutenant and returned to Japan as a buntaicho with the Kasumigaura Kokutai.

In March 1938 Aioi rejoined the 12th Kokutai as a buntaicho, it by then operating from newly captured Nanking as a specialist fighter-only unit equipped with 30 A5Ms. Subsequently seeing extensive combat over central China, Aioi participated in his first aerial combat on 29 April when he claimed to have shot down two RoCAF I-15s over Hankow. Several more engagements followed over Nanchang and Hankow during 1938, with Aioi being credited with two more victories on 26 June. In December of that same year, Aioi was transferred to the newly modernised fleet carrier *Akagi* to serve as a buntaicho for the vessel's A5M-equipped fighter unit. He briefly returned to the 12th Kokutai in October 1939, seeing more combat in southern China, prior to returning to *Akagi* in January 1940.

Postings followed to the Oita and Yokosuka Kokutais in 1940–41, but by the start of the Pacific War in December 1941, Aioi was a hikotaicho on board the light carrier *Ryujo*, where he commanded a small air group made up of A5M 'Claudes' and B5N 'Kate' bombers. On 8 December, Aioi led an unopposed strike against Davao in the southern Philippines, flying one of eight 'Claudes' acting as escorts for the 'Kates'. In February 1942 he was made hikotaicho of the 3rd Kokutai, and he would have found some familiar faces in his new unit, as many of its pilots had served alongside him with the 12th Kokutai in China. Subsequently, Aioi was heavily involved in the 1942 Darwin campaign, often leading the 3rd Kokutai in largescale aerial actions against P-40Es of the 49th FG.

After leading the 3rd Kokutai detachment to Rabaul in August 1942, Aioi, upon his return to the NEI in November, was promoted to lieutenant commander and continued to serve as CO of the newly re-designated 202nd Kokutai. On 2 March 1943, he led the daring low-level Zero-sen attack on the airfield at Coomalie Creek, and may well have briefly fought Wg Cdr Caldwell during this operation. Shortly thereafter Aioi was relieved by a new hikotaicho, and it is believed that he was among the experienced officers posted back to Japan at this time. By then he had been credited with ten aerial victories.

Subsequently, Aioi participated in the defence of the Philippines and Japan and survived the sinking of the carrier *Zuikaku* (the last surviving IJN flattop to have participated in the attack on Pearl Harbor) on 25 October 1944 during the Battle of Cape Engaño – he was rescued by an IJN destroyer. In 1954 Aioi re-joined the navy, now known as the Japanese Maritime Self-Defence Force. He duly rose to the rank of vice admiral and became Commander of the Fleet Submarine Force and then Commander-in-Chief of the Self-Defence Fleet in the 1960s. Takahide Aioi died on 6 February 1993.

Lt Takahide Aioi flew with the highly successful 12th Kokutai in China from 1937 to 1939, claiming at least four victories over RoCAF fighters in the A5M – an example of which is seen here behind him. (Tony Holmes Collection)

too was a small area that had faced relentless air attack, and in 1942 it had also been defended by Spitfire VB/Cs. No. 1 Fighter Wing was fortunate in gaining two veteran aces from this theatre. Dubbed the 'Malta twins', New South Welshmen Flg Offs Adrian 'Tim' Goldsmith and John Bisley joined No. 452 Sqn.

On New Year's Eve 1942 the first ground elements of No. 1 Fighter Wing began their move to Darwin, soon followed by the Spitfires, which flew 2,000-mile ferry flights via Mildura and Alice Springs.

While No. 1 Fighter Wing was training after months of inactivity for most of its pilots, their counterparts within the 3rd Kokutai had enjoyed little respite from combat for much of 1942. Not only had they fought the increasingly dangerous 49th FG over Darwin, more than half of the pilots assigned to the unit had then been sent to Rabaul for two months to participate in the fierce aerial clashes that were a feature of the Guadalcanal campaign. All of this combat experience in turn meant that the 3rd Kokutai worked well as a unit when engaging Allied fighters. Indeed, the tactics used by the unit as a whole were consistently superior to those employed by either the 49th FG or No. 1 Fighter Wing over Darwin.

When fighter-versus-fighter combat did develop, the P-40E and Spitfire VC pilots often showed individualistic traits. In contrast, the Japanese would fight together in small tactical formations known as shotai, typically numbering three aircraft. A common theme for Allied pilots who dared manoeuvre with a Zero-sen was quickly finding another one or two IJNAF fighters on their tail. No doubt a key factor that facilitated such flying was unit cohesion built over the long term – although qualitative changes did indeed occur to the 3rd/202nd Kokutai pilots, as will be discussed later in this chapter.

Possibly another reason why Zero-sen pilots tried to remain in tactical formation for as long as possible was their reluctance to use the aircraft's radio as a means to communicate with each other. The A6M2 had a factory-designed radio that worked well on the ground. However, the Zero-sen's unshielded engine ignition system caused electrical interference with the radio when the fighter was airborne. Furthermore, forward-deployed units often lacked the technical personnel to maintain such equipment. Finally, in order to save weight at all costs in the drive for increased endurance, Zero-sen units would usually remove weighty items such as radios. Hence, a 202nd Kokutai pilot of 1943 flew much like a World War I aviator over the Western Front, continually scanning the skies for the enemy, as well as monitoring friendly aircraft for visual signals. The long-distance flying no doubt encouraged this trait, with the Zero-sen pilots flying in the company of each other for long periods of time.

In contrast, the pilots of No. 1 Fighter Wing relied on radios for direction from ground controllers as well as from their squadron and flight leaders. There were several examples of pilots being unable to play a meaningful part in a fight after radio failure and having to return prematurely to base. Also, in large swirling dogfights involving dozens of aircraft, the effectiveness of the radios was much reduced. This was because all fighters used the same frequency, and with multiple transmissions being made at the same time, the communications became garbled and meaningless to the majority of the pilots involved. Arguably, in such situations, the Japanese pilots, used to relying on visual signals, had the upper hand.

IJNAF doctrine was to use its best aviators for combat operations, and 3rd Kokutai pilots joining the unit from March 1942 struggled to attain experience in action as a direct result of this policy. Instead, they were given secondary roles such as flying defensive combat patrols over newly acquired airfields. FPO3c Susumu Matsuki, for example, was fortunate enough to complete his flight training in September 1941 and join the 3rd Kokutai just prior to the start of the Pacific War. Nevertheless, despite three busy months of operations for the unit, Matsuki's first combat mission was the Broome raid of 3 March 1942, by which time he had flown 20 non-combat sorties. The gradual introduction into the frontline of new pilots helped to pass on the experience and ethos of the senior aviators to junior ones such as Matsuki, but it soon became unsustainable once fighter units started to experience higher rates of pilot attrition.

Between December 1941 and March 1942 the 3rd Kokutai lost 14 pilots during Southeast Asian operations. A further eight pilots (two of whom were relatively inexperienced flight school graduates) were killed in operations over northern Australia during the dry season of 1942. In September–October of that year, six more aviators perished in the Guadalcanal campaign. The total loss of 28 pilots from the 3rd/202nd Kokutai by the start of 1943 represented roughly half of the unit strength.

Furthermore, the 3rd/202nd Kokutai had also seen a significant number of experienced aviators posted elsewhere. The first pilots to leave, in April 1942, were sent to the newly formed 6th Kokutai (which was to have been based on Midway Island, following its planned capture in June), which formed with a core of veteran pilots from both the Tainan and 3rd Kokutais. Among the pilots allocated to the new

WO Shigeo Sugi-o was one of the enormously experienced pilots serving with the 202nd Kokutai during the northern Australia campaign in 1943. Prior to engaging Spitfires of No. 1 Fighter Wing, he had seen action over China, the Philippines, the NEI, Darwin (in 1942) and Guadalcanal. Sugi-o was posted back to Japan in April 1943 following near-continuous combat during the previous 18 months. (Tony Holmes Collection)

unit from the latter kokutai was Lt Zenjiro Miyano, a buntaicho with China experience who had claimed his first victory over the Philippines on the opening day of the Pacific War. Aces FPO1c Juzo Okamoto, a shotaicho and veteran of two China tours, and FPO2c Yukiharu Ozeki, also a highly experienced China veteran, were transferred to the 6th Kokutai as well. Such men were impossible to replace. Other postings followed during the course of 1942, particularly in the wake of the disastrous Battle of Midway in June of that year.

From April 1943, a number of senior pilots still serving with the 202nd Kokutai were sent back to Japan following continuous combat for at least 18 months. They had no doubt earned the right to return home, and once in Japan they served as instructors and in other senior staff roles. Among their number were Ens Fujikazu Koizumi, a shotaicho who had flown multiple missions over northern Australia in 1942–43; PO3c Kunimori Nakakariya, a veteran of the early Zero-sen missions over China; WO Shigeo Sugi-o, who had flown as a chutaicho over Guadalcanal; and Lt Sada-o Yamaguchi, who had also been a chutaicho over Guadalcanal and, in early 1943, made a number of claims against Spitfires over Darwin. All four pilots were aces.

With these changes, the quality and experience of the average 202nd Kokutai pilot certainly degraded over the course of 1942–43. By the start of 1943 the unit probably had fewer than a dozen long-service China veterans, and as noted above, from April of that year a handful of these highly experienced pilots returned to Japan. Despite this, newly arriving 202nd Kokutai pilots were inducted into a cohesive unit that had been flying on continuous combat operations for 18 months. Also, new aviators had the opportunity to fly defensive missions over their own airfield in order to gain experience. One such pilot was PO Kurakazu Goto, who was posted to the 202nd in late 1942 after graduating from flight training in July. His first victory was a B-24 he claimed on 15 February 1943 during a defensive patrol. With that experience under his belt, Goto subsequently flew three long-range escort missions over Australia between March and May 1943.

From October 1942 until August 1943, Cdr Motoharu Okamura was the CO of the 3rd/202nd Kokutai. However, this position was an administrative one, and the key flying leaders were the hikotaichos (with hiko meaning 'air' in wartime Japanese script). Lt Takahide Aioi was hikotaicho from March 1942 to March 1943, and his outstanding leadership was a major reason for the high standards achieved by the 3rd/202nd Kokutai during this period of intense action. Aioi was replaced by Lt Minoru Kobayashi, although this was probably an interim appointment as he remained in this position for only a short period of time. In April 1943 Lt Cdr Minoru Suzuki took over as hikotaicho, and he would lead the 202nd in most of its battles against No. 1 Fighter Wing.

COMBAT

Nine pilots from Nos. 452 and 457 Sqns pose with No. 1 Fighter Wing's Wing Commander Flying, Wg Cdr Clive Caldwell (wearing the white shirt in the back row) at Strauss in April 1943 – a relatively quiet month for the Spitfire units, with the enemy conducting just a handful of 'Dinah' reconnaissance flights over the Darwin area. To the right of Caldwell is ace Flg Off Adrian 'Tim' Goldsmith, who was one of two No. 452 Sqn pilots with combat experience in Spitfires over Malta. Despite this, he was forced to bail out over the sea after being hit during the controversial combat on 2 May. To the right of Goldsmith is No. 452 Sqn Flight Commander Flt Lt Ted Hall. (AWM)

In January 1943, No. 1 Fighter Wing arrived in northern Australia during the peak of the wet season. The two RAAF squadrons moved into Strauss (No. 452 Sqn) and Livingstone (No. 457 Sqn), south of Darwin, while No. 54 Sqn was sent to RAAF Base Darwin. While the Spitfire pilots acclimatised to their new hot and humid surroundings, those flying from Darwin itself got their first taste of action in-theatre when two 'Bettys' from the 753rd Kokutai targeted the airfield during the night of 20–21 January. P-40Es of Nos. 76 and 77 Sqns were still performing air defence duties at this time, and four pilots managed to attack the bombers after they were illuminated by searchlight beams. One 'Betty' was so badly damaged that it force-landed upon its return to Koepang.

A repeat attack, also by two 'Bettys', was made the following night, although on this occasion the scrambled P-40Es were unable to make contact. This was the last time that Curtiss fighters attempted to engage the enemy over Darwin, and in February, No. 1 Fighter Wing assumed

49

sole responsibility for air defence in the region. That same month No. 76 Sqn moved to Onslow, in Western Australia, and No. 77 Sqn was transferred to Milne Bay, in New Guinea.

First blood for No. 1 Fighter Wing came quickly. Around midday on 6 February, four No. 54 Sqn Spitfires intercepted a 'Dinah' reconnaissance aircraft of the 70th DCS 35 miles northwest of Cape Van Dieman. Battle of Britain veteran Flt Lt Bob Foster – one of the unit's combat-experienced flight leaders – was able to close on it as it exited the area. Approaching from dead astern, Foster fired five bursts until the Ki-46 caught fire and spiralled down into the Timor Sea.

On four other occasions in February and early March 'Dinahs' overflew the area, but cruising as high as 32,000ft, they proved elusive and no contact was made. The bombers remained absent from Darwin skies in February, with the wet weather – rather than the newly arrived Spitfires – continuing to play a key role in limiting aerial operations. However, intercepted Japanese radio traffic on 26 February indicated a formation of aircraft was moving from Kendari to the IJNAF's forward airfield at Koepang. This meant a raid was imminent and No. 1 Fighter Wing was alerted. However, a pre-emptive strike by No. 31 Sqn Beaufighters two days later proved successful, catching a number of Japanese aircraft on the ground in Timor and preventing the expected raid from being flown.

Incensed by this audacious raid, the IJNAF instructed the 202nd Kokutai to launch a counter attack as soon as possible. On 2 March, hikotaicho Lt Cdr Takahide Aioi led 21 Zero-sens from Koepang across the Timor Sea – several of the fighters were flown by junior pilots new to combat. The A6M2s were detected by radar at 1400 hrs 120 miles northwest of Darwin, and in the expectation of a normal high-level raid comprised of both fighters and bombers, 26 Spitfires were scrambled and ordered to climb for altitude as fast as they could. Aioi, however, led his formation down to low-level as they crossed the coastline and headed in the direction of the airfields south of Darwin. In doing so he avoided the Spitfires and vanished from radar contact.

At Livingstone, No. 457 Sqn ground staff had just watched 12 Spitfires scramble and head north when they were astounded to see several Zero-sens pass overhead in the opposite direction. Minutes later, the IJNAF fighters appeared at low level over the airfield at Coomalie Creek, which was home to No. 31 Sqn's Beaufighters. Aioi had achieved complete surprise, and the sole Beaufighter on the runway was strafed and destroyed. However, the remainder of the Bristol twin-engined fighters had been well dispersed and none were hit.

As the Zero-sens withdrew northwards, three of them were spotted by the ground staff of No. 452 Sqn at Strauss. These sightings were reported to the ground controller, and various Spitfires were sent in different directions in an attempt to intercept the raiders. Unsurprisingly, confusion reigned, and some No. 1 Fighter Wing pilots mistakenly reported other Spitfires as the enemy. The end result was that of the 26 aircraft scrambled, 20 were still busy searching the sky south of Darwin long after the Zero-sens had turned for home. This left a force of just six Spitfires over Darwin that were in a position to intercept the retiring Japanese fighters when they were finally re-acquired by ground controllers manning the local radar site. These aircraft were led by Wg Cdr Caldwell himself, and included Gp Capt Walters and No. 54 Sqn's CO, Sqn Ldr Gibbs.

When Caldwell finally sighted the Zero-sens at 1530 hrs, the Spitfires had been in the air for 90 minutes and had just 30 gallons of fuel remaining in their tanks. Approaching the enemy formation about 20 miles from the coast, the Spitfires were at 12,500ft when Caldwell noted six enemy aircraft below at 10,000ft (some of which were misidentified as single-engined bombers), another four Zero-sens to the left at the same altitude as the Spitfires and five more to the right and higher up at 15,000ft. Conscious of fuel limitations, Caldwell led the Spitfires in a single diving pass against the lower enemy formation, despite the danger from the Zero-sens above them. Using cloud formations to help cover their approach, it was a daring tactic by the Spitfire pilots. Wary of rear guns from the enemy 'bombers', Caldwell led his pilots in a beam attack. This set up a 90-degree deflection shot that might have been achievable for a veteran ace such as Caldwell, but it was extremely difficult for inexperienced pilots.

Leading the Spitfires in a line astern formation, Caldwell believed he had scored hits on an enemy machine before he used his speed to pull up and regain altitude. However, the top-cover Zero-sen pilots were alert to the attack. Both Walters and Gibbs found themselves under fire as they dived in, and Gibbs' aircraft was struck by three 7.7mm machine gun rounds in the engine cowling. Of the remaining three No. 54 Sqn pilots who followed, two experienced cannon failures.

The Spitfires and Zero-sens then engaged in a dogfight for several minutes. During this engagement Caldwell showed remarkable coolness under fire as he set about evaluating the relative performance of the opposing types *in combat*. After finding himself in multiple unfavourable positions, he was able to exit the combat in a full power dive. The other pilots also managed to disengage, although in retrospect they were lucky to survive having been 'bounced'. They were perhaps aided by the inexperience of some of the Japanese pilots involved, and the fact that they had already expended considerable ammunition during the attack on Coomalie Creek airfield.

Thus, the first engagement between Spitfires and Zero-sens was largely inconclusive, although two of the latter had been damaged. It says much of Caldwell's abilities that after just a few fleeting minutes of contact with the A6M2s he was able to assess their capabilities accurately. He subsequently reported that:

No. 54 Sqn pilots Flg Offs Al Mawer (left) and Bill Gregory at Darwin in April 1943. The former had shot down a Zero-sen on 15 March during a combat mission in which four Spitfires were also lost. Having claimed a Do 217 damaged over Dieppe, France, with No. 501 Sqn on 19 August 1942, Mawer, from New South Wales, was credited with two more Zero-sens destroyed and one damaged with No. 452 Sqn after joining the RAAF unit from No. 54 Sqn. He was killed during combat training on 26 September 1943 when his aircraft collided with the Spitfire VC flown by Flg Off J. P. Adam, who also perished. (AWM)

[the Spitfire] was a superior aircraft generally, though less manoeuvrable at low speeds. In straight and level flights and in the dive, the Spitfire appears faster. Though the angle of climb of the Zeke is steeper, the actual gaining of height seems the same, the Spitfire going up at a lesser angle but at a greater forward speed – an advantage. I believe that at altitudes above 20,000ft the Spitfire, in relation to the Zeke, is an even more superior aircraft.

For the next two weeks there was considerable activity over Darwin by Japanese reconnaissance aircraft – a sign that the

weather was improving as the wet season came to an end – and on 7 March another Ki-46 was shot down by two No. 457 Sqn Spitfires.

On the morning of 15 March, radar detected a plot out over the Timor Sea, but it was initially assumed to be just another reconnaissance aircraft. Twenty minutes later the formation overflew Bathurst Island, where coastwatchers quickly confirmed it was an inbound raid. Indeed, this was just about the maximum force available to the IJNAF at this time in-theatre – 19 'Betty' bombers from the 753rd Kokutai and 26 Zero-sens from the 202nd Kokutai. The initial uncertainty about the nature of the radar contact meant that the Spitfire pilots were late in scrambling. When they did finally get airborne, they were directed to rendezvous over Hughes airfield, which was mid-way between Strauss and Livingstone. The intention was to combine the wing there in line with the 'Balbo' doctrine they had been taught over previous months. While this location was convenient for Nos. 452 and 457 Sqns, it meant that No. 54 Sqn had to fly south from Darwin and away from the enemy.

On this particular morning, Wg Cdr Caldwell was getting medical treatment in Darwin and was unable to lead the wing aloft. Also in Darwin that morning were five No. 452 Sqn pilots who had been undertaking night flying training. They were in transit back to Strauss when they too were scrambled. This group was led by the No. 452 Sqn CO, Sqn Ldr Ray Thorold-Smith, who quickly assumed command of the wing in Caldwell's absence. Having expected only a short transit flight south to Strauss, the pilots' oxygen bottles had not been refilled at Darwin following the completion of their nocturnal training mission a few hours earlier.

When ground controllers advised that the enemy was fast approaching Darwin, the wing rendezvous was abandoned. Instead, various groups of Spitfires climbed as fast as possible to gain height in order to make a favourable interception. Leading was Thorold-Smith's re-routed formation from Darwin, followed by seven aircraft from No. 54 Sqn. The Spitfires were arranged in a long and ragged line governed by the speed of individual aircraft rather than any tactical formation.

As the Japanese fighters and bombers approached the entrance to Darwin Harbour off Point Charles, they were spotted by Thorold-Smith at an altitude of 23,000ft. As soon as he had a 500ft height advantage over them he attacked the bombers, although by this time two of his pilots had dropped out due to a dangerous shortage of oxygen. He was now leading just three machines against a formation of 45 heavily armed enemy aircraft. During the ensuing clash Thorold-Smith was well served by his two experienced wingmen, Flt Lt Ted Hall (a veteran of the Channel Front with the RAF's No. 129 Sqn)

The shattered remains of Spitfire BS293/QY-E at Picnic Cove on Cox Peninsula after it was shot down on 15 March. Fortunately, its pilot, Flg Off Clive 'Bill' Lloyd of No. 452 Sqn, bailed out safely. (Andrew Thomas Collection)

and Flg Off Tim Goldsmith (who would eventually become the wing's second highest scoring ace after Caldwell). After Hall warned there were fighters above, both pilots became engaged with Zero-sens and were unable to follow their leader. During this combat they saw a damaged Spitfire dive away, and they believed that this was the aircraft flown by Thorold-Smith.

Further back, the seven No. 54 Sqn pilots were also bounced by A6M2s, which attacked from above out of the blazing sun. Sgt Bert Cooper's machine was hit, and on bailing

The wingtip from the Zero-sen downed by Al Mawer on 15 March became the No. 54 Sqn scoreboard, with kills illustrated by nips of whiskey. It is seen here with eight nips in May, although actual victories were far fewer – by year-end the tally had increased to 47 and three shared kills. The No. 54 Sqn crest is on the right, while the two black swans to the left are a reference to an official gift sent from Australia to Winston Churchill. It was photographed outside the unit's readiness hut on 10 May, with Sgt W. H. Eldred pointing at the tally. Standing next to him in the pith helmet is Flg Off F. Quinn, (No. 1 Fighter Wing's Intelligence Officer), while the remaining pilots are Flg Offs J. B. Yerby (an American in the RAF), George Farries and Ian Taylor. (AWM)

out his head hit the tailplane and he was killed – his body and aircraft fell 20,000ft into Darwin Harbour. Several other No. 54 Sqn pilots managed to engage enemy machines during the ensuing dogfight, however. Flg Off Al Mawer got onto the tail of a Zero-sen and observed hits after he opened fire at short range. Mawer followed the crippled fighter as it dived away in flames and plunged into the water below, killing FPO2c Seiji Tajiri.

As these combats developed, two other sections, comprising seven Spitfires from Nos. 452 and 457 Sqns, climbed in pursuit of the 'Bettys', but they were quickly engaged by Zero-sens that forced the Australian pilots to dive away from the bombers. The No. 452 Sqn aircraft in this formation were being led by Flg Off Clive Lloyd, and his fighter received hits in the engine and wing. With oil and glycol covering his windscreen, Lloyd was forced to dive away and subsequently parachuted to safety from 5,000ft. No. 54 Sqn pilot Flt Sgt Frank Varney had also broken off combat and attempted an emergency landing adjacent to the hospital in Darwin. His aircraft landed heavily, however, and Varney died of injuries sustained in the crash. It was thought that he had been poisoned by fumes from a glycol leak, hence his efforts to attempt to land next to the hospital to obtain medical assistance.

While these fighter combats were underway, the 'Bettys' dropped their bombs with deadly accuracy and inflicted serious damage on Darwin's naval oil tanks. Maintaining their crescent formation, the aircraft then wheeled around in a 180-degree turn. Several of the Spitfires had by this point started to regain height after being engaged by the Zero-sens, and they attempted to re-acquire the bombers over the ocean as they left the target area. However, the disciplined IJNAF fighter pilots had just as quickly regained position over the 'Bettys' and a number of skirmishes ensued before the Spitfires turned for home after running very low on fuel.

There were no further casualties to either side in this running engagement over the sea, although four RAAF pilots did manage to make attacks on the bombers. In fact, the 'Betty' gunners expended 1,570 20mm cannon rounds and 10,130 7.7mm

This unidentified Spitfire VC has been carefully parked in a well-camouflaged dispersal pen at one of the new fighter airfields built south of Darwin. While much of the jungle has been cleared at ground level, trees have been used in combination with camouflage nets to create a very effective screen above the pen. (RAAF Museum)

machine gun rounds in self-defence and eight of the bombers were damaged – evidence that the four Spitfires had indeed posed a very serious threat.

After the combat had ended, Thorold-Smith failed to return to base and was posted missing, presumed killed. His Spitfire was not found until 1986, resting on the mud at the bottom of Darwin Harbour. Thorold-Smith had evidently tried to ditch his battle-damaged fighter, but with the propeller on an incorrect coarse pitch setting. Together with his poor decision-making while commencing the attack, it is speculated that the popular CO of No. 452 Sqn might have had his judgement impaired by oxygen starvation.

The actual results of the combat were three No. 1 Fighter Wing pilots killed and four Spitfires lost, with just one Zero-sen shot down in return – pilots from all three squadrons had erroneously claimed a number of IJNAF fighters and bombers destroyed in the heat of battle. Caldwell would later criticise Thorold-Smith for failing to form up the wing properly prior to engaging the IJNAF formation. Instead, Thorold-Smith had led the attack with great urgency in an apparent attempt to get at the 'Bettys' before they dropped their bombs. A further problem for No. 1 Fighter Wing was that eight of the surviving Spitfires had experienced some form of cannon failure. Also, the four pilots that had attacked the 'Bettys' had attempted to 'spray' the formation with fire rather than concentrating on a particular target. This was contrary to established doctrine. Overall, the Spitfire pilots entered combat as individuals and/or in an obsolete line astern formation. Historian Anthony Cooper provides some explanation as to why:

> In an unfortunate coincidence, all three of No. 1 Fighter Wing's squadrons and its wing leader entered the 1943 campaign with a deficient understanding of modern combat formations, and with inadequate appreciation of the cross-cover benefits this would have provided. Poor lookout and poor combat coordination were the inevitable results.

Indeed, by 1943 the 'best practice' fighter formation was to fly in line abreast in pairs and fours. Admittedly, the 202nd Kokutai still maintained an older three-aircraft 'Vee' formation at this time, although the unit had made it highly functional by keeping formed up during combat and ensuring mutual support. Strangely, in the immediate post-combat analysis of 15 March, the lack of teamwork was never deemed significant by No. 1 Fighter Wing. Nor was another factor that had quickly reared its head – the modest endurance of the Spitfire VC. After chasing the Japanese out to sea, all of the surviving No. 457 Sqn machines had returned to Livingstone 'dangerously short of fuel'.

A footnote to the 15 March combat was that a Royal Australian Navy patrol vessel was quickly able to reach the point where Tajiri's Zero-sen had crashed in Darwin Harbour. A wingtip was recovered and presented to No. 54 Sqn, becoming a treasured war trophy and the unit's scoreboard.

After the 15 March combat, No. 1 Fighter Wing did not meet Japanese aircraft again for more than six weeks. The principal reason for this lull was the launching of Operation *I-Go* by the IJNAF on 1 April. This largely unsuccessful aerial counter-offensive targeted Allied forces in the South Pacific (principally the Solomon Islands and New Guinea) in a series of bombing raids, the operation continuing until 16 April. Although neither the 202nd or the 753rd Kokutais were directly involved in *I-Go*, the latter had to cover for other units and was thinly spread, flying defensive reconnaissance missions over the NEI.

Lt Cdr Minoru Suzuki (with his right hand extended) gladly accepts sustenance at Koepang after returning from the 2 May attack on Darwin. This was his first mission to northern Australia, having only become hikotaicho of the 202nd Kokutai during the previous month. He would remain in this position until March 1944, by which time he had led most of the large-scale Zero-sen missions to northern Australia. (Tony Holmes Collection)

During this time the Spitfire pilots of No. 1 Fighter Wing were busy with a range of flying duties. This included practice scrambles, which were particularly relevant for Nos. 452 and 457 Sqns operating from the narrow bush strips at Strauss and Livingstone. The austere facilities at both sites had been persistently causing problems for pilots otherwise used to expansive British airfields, and in the first weeks of the year there had been no fewer than 29 crashes during take-offs and landings. However, from April onwards the accident rate was reduced as pilots finally got used to the local conditions.

Operational flying included sending detachments to the forward operating bases at Drysdale and on Milingimbi Island. Other duties included covering coastal shipping and undertaking army co-operation exercises, while a night detachment was also kept ready during full-moon periods. However, much of the time was spent sitting near aircraft at morning readiness, with the majority of the wing being ready to scramble in line with 'Balbo' doctrine.

From mid-April Allied reconnaissance flights over Timor detected a build-up of Japanese aircraft – the sure sign of preparations for another raid. This was accompanied by a resumption of 'Dinah' flights over Darwin. The expected raid came on 2 May, and it was a maximum effort comprising 25 'Bettys' of the 753rd Kokutai escorted by 27 Zero-sens from the 202nd Kokutai. On this occasion the A6M2s were led by the newly appointed hikotaicho, Lt Cdr Minoru Suzuki.

The radar station at Cape Fourcroy, on Bathurst Island, detected the incoming formation at 0935 hrs and No. 1 Fighter Wing was duly scrambled. This time Wg Cdr Caldwell led the Spitfires aloft, with 34 of them rendezvousing overhead Hughes at 10,000ft. With the aircraft formed up by 1000 hrs, Caldwell deployed his three squadrons in line abreast and climbed for altitude as he led them to an up-sun

With flak bursts trailing in their wake, 'Betty' bombers of the 753rd Kokutai fly over Darwin during the morning of 2 May 1943. This was a maximum effort raid by 25 G4M1s, but their bombs fell mostly wide of RAAF Base Darwin and only light damage was inflicted. Above and behind the high-flying bombers are some of the 27 A6M2/3s that escorted the 'Bettys' on the raid. Although the 753rd Kokutai suffered no casualties, several 'Bettys' were damaged. (Bob Alford)

position ten miles northeast of Darwin. As Caldwell passed through 16,000ft to the east of Darwin, he was advised that the enemy formation was over the west side of Darwin Harbour at 25,000ft and still climbing. Determined not to repeat Thorold-Smith's mistake of 15 March, Caldwell decided not to attack without an altitude advantage, even if it meant engaging the enemy after the bombers had dropped their ordnance. This allowed the 'Bettys' to make an uncontested bombing run on RAAF Base Darwin at 26,000ft, with their Zero-sen top-cover flying at an astonishing 31,000ft – very close to their maximum ceiling.

It was a bright, clear day, and the 'Betty' formation was plainly visible from the ground below, trailed by dozens of bursts of anti-aircraft gun fire as the bombs were dropped over RAAF Base Darwin at 1015 hrs. However, attacking from such a high altitude entailed a considerable sacrifice in respect to accuracy. The bombs fell across the southern edge of the base, with most of them exploding harmlessly in the bush.

As Caldwell continued to gain altitude, the enemy formation turned right and initially retired in a southwesterly direction. Two Spitfires had been forced to break off the pursuit due to mechanical problems during the full-power climb, so Caldwell led 31 pilots evenly distributed between the three squadrons (ten from No. 54 Sqn, eleven from No. 452 Sqn and ten from No. 457 Sqn). Flying at 33,000ft, he manoeuvred the wing so that it was on a parallel track to the enemy formation. However, the 'Bettys' now adopted their standard post-bombing tactic of going into a shallow dive in order to gain speed. Not wanting to lose the tactical advantage of his own superior altitude, Caldwell could only pursue the enemy at a modest speed due to fuel considerations. The chase was slow as a result, with the Spitfires only closing at a mile per minute. By the time they overtook the enemy, Caldwell had maintained a height advantage of 10,000ft, but the Spitfires were now well out to sea.

Although No. 54 Sqn was lagging, its pilots were ordered by the wing leader to attack a formation of Zero-sens flying behind the bombers. Caldwell intended for the remaining two squadrons to engage the 'Betty' formation. The attack finally commenced some 60 miles out to sea, the Spitfires diving steeply from high altitude. Within a few moments four pilots had experienced CSU failures due to oil congealing at such high ceilings. Fortunately, all of them survived (three bailed out and one crash-landed), but four Spitfires were out of the fight just as it began.

SPITFIRE VC COCKPIT

1. Boost control cut-out
2. Brake triple pressure gauge
3. Elevator tabs position indicator
4. Undercarriage position indicator
5. Oxygen regulator
6. Flaps control
7. Blind flying instrument panel
8. Lifting ring for sun screen
9. Reflector gunsight switch
10. Sun screen
11. Gun and cannon three-position push button
12. Camera-gun push button (for activation)
13. Barr and Stroud GM-2 reflector gunsight
14. Voltmeter
15. Ventilator control
16. Tachometer
17. Fuel pressure warning lamp
18. Boost pressure gauge
19. Oil pressure gauge
20. Oil temperature gauge
21. Radiator temperature gauge
22. Fuel contents gauge and push button
23. Remote contactor and contactor switch
24. Slow-running cut-out
25. Engine priming pump
26. Engine starting push button
27. Booster coil push button
28. Fuel cock control
29. Rudder pedals
30. Radiator flap control lever
31. Two-position door catch
32. Cockpit floodlight
33. Camera indicator supply plug
34. Navigation lights switch
35. Control friction adjusters
36. Propeller speed control lever
37. Radio controller plug stowage
38. Elevator trimming tab handwheel
39. Camera-gun switch
40. Map case
41. Pitot tube head heater switch
42. Rudder trimming tab handwheel
43. Oil dilution push button
44. Stowage for reflector gunsight lamps
45. Signalling switchbox
46. R.3002 Identification Friend or Foe (IFF) master push buttons
47. Harness release control
48. R.3002 IFF master switch
49. CO_2 cylinder for emergency lowering of undercarriage
50. Oxygen supply cock
51. Windscreen de-icing pump
52. Windscreen de-icing needle valve
53. Undercarriage emergency lowering control
54. Windscreen de-icing cock
55. Drop tank jettison lever
56. Undercarriage control unit lever
57. Rudder pedal adjusting starwheels
58. Ignition switches
59. Signal discharger control
60. T.R. 1196 or T.R. 1304 high-frequency transmitter/receiver controls
61. Fuel tank pressurisation cock control
62. Air intake control
63. Throttle control
64. Pilot's seat
65. Oxygen hose
66. Airspeed indicator
67. Artificial horizon
68. Rate-of-climb indicator
69. Altimeter
70. Turn-and-slip indicator

Flg Off Tim Goldsmith was already a high-scoring Malta ace, with both a DFM and DFC to his name, by the time he joined No. 452 Sqn in February 1943. Indeed, he was No. 1 Fighter Wing's second ranking ace after Wg Cdr Caldwell. Claiming a 'Hamp' and a 'Betty' destroyed (and a second 'Hamp' damaged) on 15 March, Goldsmith was credited with downing another 'Betty' on 2 May, although he too was forced to take to his parachute moments later when his Spitfire was hit while diving away from Zero-sens – usually a safe manoeuvre in the heavier Spitfire. (Andrew Thomas Collection)

In the case of No. 54 Sqn, the high-speed dive against the Zero-sens presented the pilots with difficult high-deflection shots, after which a dogfight developed at 18,000ft. Plt Off George Farries fired at enemy fighters on four separate occasions, but in his eagerness he failed to check his tail and was hit from behind by both 20mm and 7.7mm rounds. As his engine seized up, Farries dived away, but he was too far out to sea to glide back to land. He bailed out and spent five hours in a dinghy before being rescued.

A short distance ahead, No. 457 Sqn began a similar high-speed high-angle dive attack on the bombers. However, only one section succeeded in firing on the 'Bettys' before Zero-sens managed to break up the formation. Some of the Spitfire pilots experienced fogged-up canopies in their quick descent, and Flg Off Gordon Gifford was shot down and killed after possibly suffering such a loss of forward vision.

Meanwhile, Caldwell himself led No. 452 Sqn's attack, also in a steep dive, through a Zero-sen formation to reach the 'Bettys'. Tim Goldsmith was able to make a shallower approach and fired from close range into a bomber. However, like several pilots on this day, he experienced single cannon failure and then found that he had been bounced by Zero-sens. Goldsmith chose to exit the combat through a fast rolling dive – a technique he had used with great success on numerous occasions when being pursued by German and Italian pilots over Malta. However, on this occasion, a Zero-sen followed him through the dive and skilfully executed a difficult shot against Goldsmith's manoeuvring aircraft. With his controls severed, the ace was lucky to bail out successfully just as his aircraft broke up around him.

As Spitfires pulled out of their dives, Zero-sens swarmed around them. Caldwell's own wingman suffered a total armament failure and returned to base. All six guns had frozen up, and investigations found that no gun heating system of any kind had been installed in that particular aircraft. Plt Off Ken Fox latched onto a Zero-sen he saw getting onto Caldwell's tail and fired at it. He had not seen another A6M2 flying cover on the first, however, and he was hit and forced to bail out.

Overall, a running dogfight was fought over the sea that lasted around fifteen minutes. As detailed above, four Spitfires were lost in combat, with a fifth crashing in unknown circumstances (killing Flg Off A. C. McNab of No. 452 Sqn), four more falling to engine failure and five to fuel starvation. Not a single Zero-sen was lost in return, although seven were damaged to some degree – the Spitfire pilots claimed four destroyed and five probables, along with a 'Betty' as a probable also.

Generally, the 202nd Kokutai had been effective in defending the bombers from attack by No. 1 Fighter Wing. Indeed, just five Spitfire pilots reported firing at the bombers. No 'Bettys' were lost, although eight were damaged, and the bomber gunners expended 1,020 20mm and 9,500 7.7mm rounds in self-defence. Not for the only time in 1943, many Japanese aircrew were probably saved by Spitfire cannon failures in this instance. Of the 11 pilots who fired their guns and made claims against both Zero-sens and 'Bettys', only two did not experience gun stoppage problems.

At 1036 hrs, Caldwell broadcast a warning for pilots to check their fuel and to immediately return to base. Some of the Spitfires were now 80 miles or more from Darwin and critically short of fuel. Of those pilots that did make it back to base, most landed between 1110 and 1125 hrs with near-empty tanks. Five Spitfires were lost due to fuel exhaustion – one ditched and four force-landed. In retrospect, it is difficult to understand why the Spitfires had flown without drop tanks on 2 May, particularly as the earlier combats had already indicated a problem with the limited endurance of the fighters. Drop tanks were subsequently carried, these holding 30 gallons of fuel which gave an extra hour of flying time at normal cruising speed.

On this day No. 1 Fighter Wing had lost 14 aircraft, or almost 50 per cent of the strength of those that fought the action. Indeed, the Japanese believed they had inflicted significant losses on the Spitfire force, with the 6 May 1943 edition of the *Nippon Times* featuring the headline 'Port Darwin Raid Terrifies Anzacs' and the accompanying report noting:

> Poor show of Spitfires causes heated discussions – blame is put on bad weather. The question of why the Spitfires, considered by the anti-Axis camp to be the best fighter plane in the world, failed to show their power in air combats in the May 2 raid has become the centre of much heated discussion in Australia.

On the Allied side, the losses caused much controversy and criticism of No. 1 Fighter Wing, including from senior American officers. These high losses continued to be associated with the 'Darwin Spitfire' story for many years. In 1995, Caldwell himself wrote dryly:

> Any mention of Spitfires at Darwin usually brings the sort of stupid response 'Oh yes, didn't they get the hell beaten out of them by the Japs' or 'they all fell into the sea out of petrol or something'.

At the time, the reaction within No. 1 Fighter Wing to the events of 2 May was more pragmatic and less catastrophic, probably because only two pilots had been killed despite the loss of so many Spitfires. There is little doubt that the Spitfire VCs were hampered by technical difficulties at high altitude, particularly in relation to CSU and gun failures. Also, it can be argued that Caldwell's 'Balbo' tactics used up excessive fuel in forming up and then positioning for the attack. Quite simply, the Spitfires did not have the endurance for such tactics. However, in the face of criticism, Caldwell was reluctant to forgo what he saw as the fundamental advantage of a full-wing interception.

MILINGIMBI ISLAND

Some 300 miles east of Darwin was Milingimbi Island, on which the RAAF had established an Advanced Operational Base. Consisting of little more than a cleared airstrip and a dump of fuel drums, Milingimbi was used by the RAAF to provide anti-submarine cover

Veteran fighter pilot Ens Fujikazu Koizumi engaged Spitfires on a handful of occasions prior to returning to Japan in May 1943 after 18 months in the frontline. He had initially seen combat over central China with the 12th Kokutai in 1937, claiming the first of his 13 victories in February of the following year. Assigned to the 3rd Kokutai in September 1941, Koizumi was one of the unit's shotai leaders during the attack on Luzon on 8 December that same year – he claimed a number of USAAC aircraft shot down over Clark Field, on Luzon, two days later. Subsequently involved in the invasion of the NEI, Koizumi also took part in attacks on Darwin and Wyndham in 1942. Following his return to Japan, and a brief spell as an instructor, he flew Zero-sens from the carrier *Hiyo*. Koizumi was sent with the rest of the carrier air group to Vunakanau airfield, Rabaul, in January 1944, and he was posted missing in action shortly thereafter. (Tony Holmes Collection)

Ace FPO1c Yoshiro Hashiguchi flew as wingman to several 202nd Kokutai hikotaicho, including Lt Cdr Minoru Suzuki, prior to returning to Japan in mid-1943. A China veteran with the 12th Kokutai, Hashiguchi had joined the 3rd Kokutai in November 1941. Seeing action over the Philippines and the NEI, he also took part in raids on Darwin from April to August 1942, when he was sent to Rabaul. Hashiguchi returned to northern Australian skies in 1943 with the 202nd Kokutai. (Tony Holmes Collection)

for Allied vessels sailing in the nearby Arafura Sea and to act as a staging base for RAAF Hudsons and Beaufighters harassing Japanese forces in the islands to the north. On 9 May, seven 'Bettys' from the 753rd Kokutai bombed Milingimbi just before midday. In response, six No. 457 Sqn Spitfires were forward deployed to the airstrip from Darwin that afternoon.

This move proved to be fortuitous, as across the Arafura Sea at Langgoer, in the Kai Islands, the 202nd Kokutai had also forward deployed nine fighters (including some A6M3 'Hamps') on 9 May. The next day they took off on a strafing attack against Milingimbi, the formation being led by veteran pilot Lt Morio Myaguchi. He had graduated from flying school in 1933 and had subsequently spent a number of years flying fighters from carriers. As the Zero-sens approached Milingimbi at 12,000ft, they were detected by the No. 308 Radar Station at a distance of less than 12 miles.

Five Spitfires were then in the process of landing after investigating an earlier plot that had proved to be two incoming Beaufighters. Because of this, each aircraft made a maximum power climb with the intention of regaining formation at altitude. Expecting another bomber raid, the appearance of nine Zero-sens took the Spitfire pilots by surprise. The RAAF fighters were caught while still climbing, making them vulnerable to attack. In the ensuing dogfight, the Zero-sens fought in their customary three-aircraft shotais, although on this occasion the IJNAF pilots failed to score critical hits during the initial bounce. As individual Spitfires tried to shake off pursuing A6Ms in high-speed dives, two suffered CSU failures.

A confused low-level dogfight then ensued as the Zero-sens came down to strafe the airfield – one Beaufighter was destroyed on the ground. Plt Off Bruce Little's Spitfire was damaged and he subsequently crashed into a dry salt pan during the low-level melee. Despite the speed of the impact, he somehow survived unhurt. During this engagement the No. 457 Sqn pilots fought back in a spirited fashion, even though they had been forced to scrap with the Zero-sens at an altitude that allowed the Japanese fighters to take full advantage of their superior manoeuvrability. The

202nd Kokutai lost two aircraft to the plucky Australian pilots, with one Zero-sen diving into the sea during combat and the other crashing during the return flight to Langgoer. Both pilots were shotaicho, PO1C Kunio Sakai being killed in action and future ace PO1C Tadao Yamanaka surviving the ditching to be rescued.

The strength of the Milingimbi detachment was soon upgraded to eight Spitfires, with the three squadrons taking it in turns to operate from the airstrip. On 28 May, while No. 457 Sqn was again performing this role, nine 'Bettys' escorted by seven Zero-sens bombed Milingimbi from 23,000ft. Despite their uninterrupted approach, the aircraft dropped their ordnance wide of the runway and the bombs exploded harmlessly in the bush. By then, seven Spitfires had scrambled, and they began to reach the 'Bettys'' altitude shortly after they had made their first bombing run on the airstrip. On this day there was a thick layer of haze at medium altitude that restricted visibility. Partly because of this, the Spitfires made their climbs individually. Two relatively junior pilots, Flg Offs Tommy Clark and Warwick Turner, were the first to intercept the bombers. Attacking separately, they were

The salvaged remains of Spitfire VC BS199/ZP-S of No. 457 Sqn, which Plt Off Bruce Little crashed into a dry salt pan during a low-level melee with Zero-sens over Milingimbi Island on 10 May 1943. Despite the speed of the impact, Little emerged from the wreckage unscathed. (Peter R. Arnold Collection)

both quickly bounced by multiple Zero-sens and wisely dived away. However, this meant that the bombers were now unescorted, as the 202nd Kokutai pilots lost altitude chasing Clark and Turner.

Possibly unaware of the presence of the Spitfires because of the thick haze, the leader of the 'Betty' formation turned to make a second and then a third bombing run over Milingimbi. During these passes several of the Spitfires pressed home attacks on the 'Bettys', despite three of the fighters being damaged by potentially lethal 20mm fire from the rear gunners. At least 15 firing passes were made, and the Spitfire pilots were rewarded by seeing three 'Bettys' drop out of formation with evidence of damage.

Although initially lured away, the Zero-sen escorts were soon able to regroup and shoot down two of the Spitfires – Flg Offs F. B. Blake and A. H. Beale were killed. Two 'Bettys' had indeed been shot down, with the loss of 15 crew, a third bomber was forced to ditch during the return flight (its crew was rescued), while a fourth forced-landed and was written off.

IJAAF RAID

Following the controversial engagement on 2 May, the only Japanese aircraft seen in the skies over Darwin for the next six weeks were 'Dinahs'. These reconnaissance flights detected a large build-up of stores, vehicles and equipment at Winnellie, a suburb in northern Darwin near the town's airfield. This material was for the newly arrived USAAF 380th Bomb Group (BG), equipped with B-24 Liberators. The Japanese were determined to mount a strike while the equipment was vulnerable – it would soon be camouflaged and dispersed at another of the airfields to the south called Fenton.

However, the 202nd and 753rd Kokutais were busy elsewhere at this time, and in a rare example of inter-service co-operation, the IJAAF stepped in for what would be its only raid on Darwin. The strike was mounted by 18 Ki-49 'Helens' of the 61st Sentai and nine Ki-48 'Lilys' of the 75th Sentai, escorted by 22 Ki-43 'Oscar' fighters of the 59th Sentai.

LEFT
Eleven cherry blossom victory symbols adorn the tail of FP01c Yoshiro Hashiguchi's Zero-sen (manufactured in November 1941) at Koepang in 1942. (Tony Holmes Collection)

Future ace PO1c Tadao Yamanaka gained his first combat experience during the Milingimbi Island raid on 10 May, and he survived ditching his fighter into the sea on the return leg to Langgoer. He would participate in at least five more missions over northern Australia prior to transferring to the 204th Kokutai with a number of other pilots from the 202nd in December 1943. Subsequently seeing action over Rabaul, Bougainville and New Guinea, Yamanaka also took part in the defence of Truk in 1944 and Okinawa in 1945 (with the 210th Kokutai). Based in the home islands at the end of the war, his final official tally was nine victories. (Tony Holmes Collection)

During this period there had been much discussion within No. 1 Fighter Group's leadership about its relatively poor performance to date. The result was a memo on Spitfire tactics, the main points of which were:

- Pilots should concentrate on relatively easy low-deflection gunnery attacks
- Manoeuvring with Zero-sen was to be avoided
- Dive and zoom attacks were preferred
- Numerical disadvantages were acceptable as the Spitfire had the speed to disengage when necessary
- Short engagements were necessary because of limited endurance
- Line abreast fours would be the new tactical formation

However, Caldwell's preference for 'Balbo' interceptions remained, even given the precious time spent forming up.

The IJAAF raid came on 20 June, and was initially plotted by operators of No. 38 Radar Station at Cape Fourcroy at 0945 hrs. The attacks mounted by the IJNAF had usually made a western approach to Darwin, but on this occasion the IJAAF pilots crossed over Bathurst and Melville Islands before turning south to approach Darwin from the northeast. Because of this different track, the first interceptions were made before the bombers reached the target area. Caldwell was once again leading the wing, but while it was forming up his radio became unserviceable. Command was subsequently handed over to No. 457 Sqn's Flt Lt Pete Watson, who quickly recognised that a full wing rendezvous was impractical. Instead, each squadron climbed independently, which was much faster than climbing in wing formation.

With its more northerly base, No. 54 Sqn was the first to engage the attackers. However, of 16 Spitfires that scrambled from RAAF Base Darwin, three aborted due to mechanical failures and at least two others had underperforming engines. Nonetheless, No. 54 Sqn found the 'Helen' formation – comprising six three-aircraft Vs – just south of Melville Island flying at 25,000ft, with most of the Spitfires in an ideal attacking position of up to 5,000ft above the Ki-49s. Also visible was the heavy escort of 'Oscars', dispersed on the flanks of the bomber formation.

In the ensuing attack, Flg Off Tony Hughes fired into one of the lead bombers on the port side, getting to within close range of his target. The 'Helen' soon burst into flames and dropped out of formation. However, Hughes' aircraft had also been damaged by return fire and his engine seized. Fortunately, he was able to glide back to a beach and make a successful belly landing.

No. 452 Sqn was commanded by newly appointed Sqn Ldr Ron MacDonald (who had replaced Thorold-Smith). MacDonald led an attack against the tightly packed enemy formation, with his pilots reporting thick defensive fire. However, the attack was mired by gun failures, with six No. 452 Sqn pilots subsequently stating that both cannons had jammed on this day. Nevertheless, Malta ace Flg Off John Bisley made a successful stern attack on a 'Helen', noticing the starboard engine burning before his cannons jammed. This machine was then seen spinning down in flames with the outer wings snapped off, and the wreckage was found at Koolpinyah Station.

Stung into action, the 'Oscar' pilots quickly came to the defence of the remaining bombers. Bisley duly found himself under fire, and after a series of violent manoeuvres that shook off his opponent, he could not see his wingman, Flt Sgt Tony Ruskin-Rowe, either. The wreckage of the latter's Spitfire was found three weeks later ten miles north of Koolpinyah Station. He had been struck in the head by a single 12.7mm round fired from an 'Oscar'.

Meanwhile, Flg Off Al Mawer had led two other Spitfires in an attack against two 'Oscars'. During this engagement, one of the Ki-43s suffered a catastrophic wing failure after it was hit by 20mm cannon rounds – as evidenced by Mawer's gun camera film. The 'Oscar' crashed into the sea, followed shortly thereafter by the No. 452 Sqn aircraft flown by the relatively inexperienced Plt Off W. E. Nichterlein, who was killed. He was almost certainly another victim of the Ki-43s.

Although Nos. 54 and 452 Sqns had intercepted the IJAAF formation without any trouble, No. 457 Sqn had experienced difficulty in locating the enemy aircraft, despite hearing evolving combats over the radio. Of 13 Spitfires sent aloft by the unit, one section of four investigated some aircraft seen at low level (which proved to be RAAF Catalinas) and were unable to re-enter the fight. The remaining No. 457 Sqn pilots finally closed on the enemy bombers as they approached RAAF Base Darwin. The squadron's effectiveness was further reduced by the now customary CSU and cannon failures. Its pilots were also forced to make fast, steep-angle diving attacks that resulted in them having to take difficult high-deflection shots. These were probably ineffective, although some hits were claimed as the Spitfires zoomed through the 'Helen' formation.

At 1043 hrs the Ki-49s released their bombs, which landed accurately among the 380th BG stores park at Winnellie on the edge of RAAF Base Darwin. Two servicemen were killed and 13 wounded, and a modest amount of damage was inflicted. Minutes later, nine 'Lilys' arrived overhead at low altitude, strafing the airfield and dropping their own bombs. The IJAAF pilots had carried out a well-coordinated high- and low-level attack. Indeed, the Ki-48s had approached unnoticed at wave-top height over the sea, avoiding detection until they were virtually over the target area. This element of the raid had caught much of No. 1 Fighter Wing flat-footed, leaving Spitfires to hunt the 'Lilys' down as they fled north. However, only five ineffective attacks were made, the bombers maintaining a very tight formation at low altitude over the sea that maximised their mutual defensive firepower and narrowed the attack options of the Spitfire pilots. All of the Ki-48s returned to their base in Timor.

While this ultimately fruitless pursuit was taking place, almost a dozen Spitfires had re-climbed after their various diving attacks on the 'Helens' and were able to re-position themselves to attack the remaining Ki-49s, still flying at 20,000ft and also battling their way back home. However, cannon failures continued to bedevil No. 1 Fighter Wing. Another factor that caused the defending pilots problems was the unfamiliar shape and dark green camouflage of the 'Oscars' (in contrast to the overall light grey of the 202nd Kokutai Zero-sens), which caused some to confuse them with Spitfires.

Flt Sgt Rex Watson of No. 457 Sqn engaged Japanese aircraft on five occasions during 1943 and made six claims – two 'Zekes' destroyed and one damaged, a share in the destruction of a 'Dinah' and two 'Bettys' damaged. Born in Devon but raised in New South Wales, Watson was later commissioned and flew with No. 452 Sqn. He has personalised his 'Mae West' through the addition of *Jiminy Cricket* artwork. (Andrew Thomas Collection)

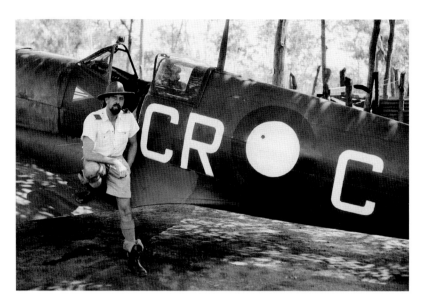

A bearded Wg Cdr Clive Caldwell, complete with his pipe, unzipped flying boots and piratical beard, which he grew because the tropical heat caused a skin irritation, poses with his Spitfire VC, BS295. By the time this photograph was taken in June 1943, No. 1 Fighter Wing's Wing Commander Flying had had his aircraft marked with the codes 'CR-C', for Clive Robertson Caldwell. All other No. 1 Fighter Wing Spitfires flew with their squadron fuselage codes and a third identification letter. Caldwell had claimed his first success over the IJNAF in this aircraft on 2 March, and he also flew it during two raids in late June when he was credited with shooting down two Zero-sens and probably destroying two 'Betty' bombers. Note the wing commander's pennant to the left of Caldwell's head. (AWM)

Overall, No. 1 Fighter Wing had done well to make more than 30 individual firing passes on the bombers, and evidence suggests that two 'Helens' were definitely shot down and a third force-landed in Timor. However, like the Zero-sen pilots, their brethren flying Ki-43s that day had proven skilful in protecting the bombers.

On both 21 and 22 June, formations of 'Oscars' made flights over the Timor Sea towards Darwin, but these proved to be feints. However, a reconnaissance flight by a 'Dinah' on 27 June proved to be the precursor to the return of IJNAF aircraft over the area the following day. This time the attack comprised just nine 'Bettys' of the 753rd Kokutai, with a strong escort of 27 Zero-sens from the 202nd Kokutai. The raid was detected well out to sea on the normal westerly track used by the IJNAF. A total of 42 Spitfires were scrambled (although two soon aborted due to mechanical trouble), and they made a full wing rendezvous over Sattler airstrip before proceeding to climb to 30,000ft. No. 452 Sqn was late, however, and lagged behind the remaining two squadrons in the climb.

No. 54 Sqn was the first to spot the nine 'Bettys' at the impressive height of 27,000ft, with fighters arranged above them in several groups – not all of which were visible to any given Spitfire formation. The CO of No. 54 Sqn, Sqn Ldr Bill Gibbs, believed he was in an advantageous position and requested permission to attack. This was denied by Caldwell, who was waiting for No. 452 Sqn to catch up in order to arrange a 'Balbo' interception.

As a result of this delay, the 753rd Kokutai bombers once again arrived over the target prior to being intercepted, and their bombs inflicted damage on the East Point coastal defence installations. As usual after their bombing run, the 'Bettys' pointed their noses down and gained speed as they exited the area. Together with a slight change of course, this spoiled Caldwell's attack plans as he stalked the enemy on a roughly parallel course. It also meant No. 452 Sqn was now some 15 miles distant. Meanwhile, No. 54 Sqn also lagged behind after taking evasive measures against a section of Spitfires they mistakenly thought were Zero-sens (the offending section had been out of position due to underperforming engines). Further course changes wrongly anticipated the enemy's position, with the result that both Nos. 54 and 452 Sqns frustratingly returned to base without encountering the enemy.

So it was that No. 457 Sqn was left to make the attack alone, the bombers now at 23,000ft and 14 Spitfires at 31,000ft. In the ensuing combat, two sections of nine RAAF fighters attacked a formation of Zero-sens while five Spitfires engaged the

A6M2 ZERO-SEN COCKPIT

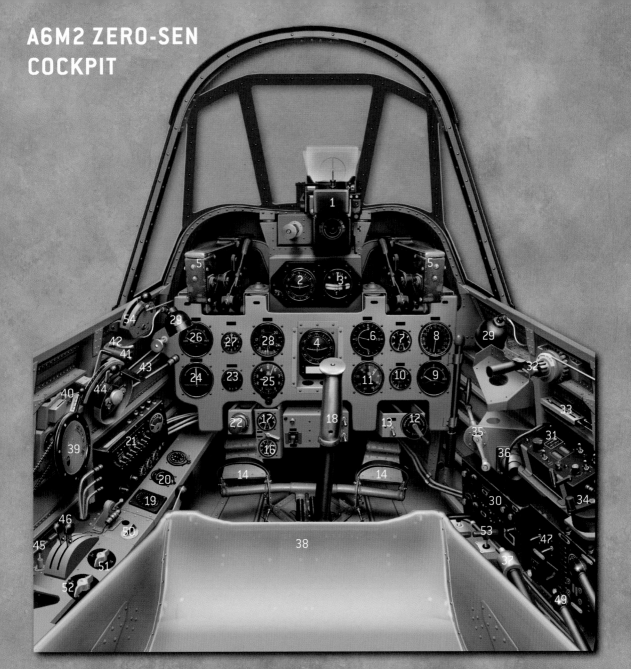

1. IJNAF Type 98 Reflector Gunsight
2. Artificial horizon
3. Turn-and-slip indicator
4. Compass
5. IJNAF Type 97 7.7mm machine guns
6. Rate-of-climb indicator
7. Fuel pressure gauge
8. Tachometer
9. Cylinder temperature gauge
10. Oil temperature gauge
11. Intake manifold pressure gauge
12. Oil cooler shutter control handle
13. Ignition plug charger switch
14. Rudder/brake pedals
15. Oxygen control
16. Oxygen pressure gauge
17. Oxygen quantity gauge
18. Control column
19. Wing fuel tanks quantity gauge
20. Fuselage fuel tank quantity gauge
21. Switchboard
22. Fuel injection pump
23. Engine main switch
24. Radio direction indicator
25. Altimeter
26. Exhaust temperature gauge
27. Clock
28. Airspeed indicator
29. Interior lights
30. Radio homing control unit
31. Type 3 Mk 1 radio control panel
32. Arrestor hook retraction handle
33. Arrestor hook/flaps down angle indicator
34. Radio homing equipment control lever
35. Cowl gills control handle
36. Cockpit ventilation air intake
37. Seat adjustment lever
38. Seat
39. Elevator trim tab control handle
40. Machine gun safety lever
41. Throttle lever
42. Machine gun selector switch
43. Propeller pitch adjustment lever
44. Mixture control lever
45. Drop tank release lever
46. Bomb release lever
47. Switchboard
48. Flap control
49. Landing gear lever
50. Drop tank selector gauge
51. Fuselage/wing tanks switching cock
52. Wing tanks selector lever
53. Emergency gear down lever
54. High-altitude automatic mixture control

Sqn Ldr Bill Gibbs' Spitfire VC BS164/DL-K is wheeled back into its camouflaged bay on 22 June shortly after the IJAAF had attacked Darwin – note that the groundcrew are all wearing steel helmets. Five days later Gibbs had No. 54 Sqn in an advantageous position over a formation of 'Bettys' while flying this aircraft, but he was denied permission to attack by Caldwell who was trying to form up the entire wing. Gibbs would claim three 'Zekes' and one 'Betty' destroyed, two 'Bettys' probably destroyed and one 'Zeke' and one 'Betty' damaged in BS164 during four engagements with the IJNAF. (AWM)

A Zero-sen 72-gallon drop tank is retrieved from the sea off Darwin on 28 June by sailors from a naval vessel. No A6M2s were downed over land in 1943, and only drop tanks and the wingtip used as a scoreboard by No. 54 Sqn were ever recovered from the water. (AWM)

bombers. However, those attacking the A6M2s soon found themselves bounced by more Zero-sens. Two Spitfires suffered combat damage while another crash-landed after a CSU failure. Just two No. 457 Sqn pilots were able to make five attacks on the bombers, one of which was clearly seen to lose altitude while trailing smoke. This was prior to the intervention by the Zero-sen pilots, who, with their usual exemplary teamwork, forced the outnumbered Spitfires to break off the engagement. On this occasion one 'Betty' was lost when it crash-landed at Lautem, in Timor.

The next Japanese raid occurred just two days later, on 30 June. This time it was a maximum strength effort, although the 753rd Kokutai could now put only 23 'Bettys' into the air. They were accompanied again by a strong escort of 27 A6M2s from the 202nd Kokutai. The reason for the attack was the discovery by 'Dinah' reconnaissance flights of the 380th BG base at Fenton, 80 miles to the south of Darwin. It would duly become the southernmost location to be bombed since early 1942. The raid was picked up by radar at 1118 hrs while still some distance out over the Timor Sea, and 39 Spitfires were scrambled, again led by Caldwell. This time the deep penetration track of the enemy better suited the 'Big Wing' tactics, for it allowed ample time to form up. After the intruders crossed the coast at 25,000ft, they were spotted by Caldwell at a distance of around 12 miles from the wing, which had by then climbed to 32,000ft.

Caldwell directed the Spitfires to close on the Japanese formation while maintaining a slight altitude advantage over the Zero-sens. However, No. 1 Fighter Wing was flying a single compact formation that was easily spotted by the enemy, thus enabling their smaller fighter formations to take up positions from where they could block any attacking move by the Spitfires. Caldwell then directed Nos. 54 and 457 Sqns to attack the bombers in a pincer movement from the left and right sides, respectively, while No. 452 Sqn would take on the fighters. The problem was, for such attacks to take place simultaneously, more manoeuvring was required. This took up more time and fuel, and on this particular day many of the Spitfires were flying without drop tanks as there was a shortage of them.

ENGAGING THE ENEMY

A No. 1 Fighter Wing pilot flames an A6M2 during the 1943 Darwin air campaign. Most of the engagements between the Spitfire VCs and Zero-sens occurred on the Japanese return leg (over the Timor Sea) after the targets had already been bombed. Typically, Spitfire pilots used up time and precious fuel attempting a full wing interception of the intruders from high altitude. After making fast diving attacks against the 'Betty' bombers, many of the pilots then got caught up in dogfights with the escorting Zero-sens, despite limited fuel and often malfunctioning armament. No doubt a number of Japanese pilots owed their lives to the unreliability of the Spitfire's Hispano 20mm cannon – their lightly built and unarmoured Zero-sens were unlikely to have survived being hit by such large-calibre rounds.

It was common for Spitfire pilots to report smoking engines as evidence for their claims against Zero-sens. However, the A6M2/3's engine had a habit of emitting smoke when full combat power was applied. The lack of supporting wreckage (and other evidence) should have been a factor in limiting such claims – just a single wingtip was the sole Zero-sen wreckage recovered during the entire 1943 campaign.

While No. 1 Fighter Wing's Intelligence Officer, Flg Off F. Quinn, argued in favour of properly using RAF Air Ministry criteria to confirm each kill claim, it seems the political pressure for the wing to be successful was such that lax standards were applied at the time.

Also, as many as 11 fighters were affected by various technical problems, and there were a variety of aborts both before and during the action. To add to the difficulties already plaguing No. 1 Fighter Wing, after six months of operations, many Spitfires had worn engines, resulting in their performance being far below what it had been earlier in the year.

As Nos. 54 and 457 Sqns made their pincer attack, it seems this was easily read by the defending Zero-sens. As the leaders zoomed into the Japanese bomber formation, the IJNAF fighter pilots got onto the tail of some of the trailing Spitfires. Sqn Ldr Bill Gibbs once again led No. 54 Sqn, and claimed hits on a bomber. However, as he looked back 'a fleeting glimpse on passing through showed enemy fighters closing in'. Indeed, the No. 54 Sqn pilots' fixation on the bombers had allowed the Zero-sen pilots to spring a successful ambush. Three Spitfires were shot down, with Flg Off J. C. Wellsman being killed. Another No. 54 Sqn machine was hit by return fire from the bombers and the pilot bailed out. In return, the squadron managed 13 gunnery passes against the bombers, but pilots were bedevilled by the usual gun failures that affected virtually every aircraft.

A short time after No. 54 Sqn engaged the bombers, nine Spitfires from No. 452 Sqn dived into the melee from 6,000ft above the IJNAF formation. This led to an extremely fast closing speed – an attack profile which had not been overly successful in previous engagements. Furthermore, as with the aircraft of No. 54 Sqn, all of No. 452 Sqn's Spitfires suffered some form of gun failure, resulting in its attack probably failing to inflict any significant damage on the 'Bettys'. The unit also suffered the day's second fatality when Flg Off W. J. Lamerton crashed while trying to force-land his Spitfire at Strauss. He subsequently died of burns inflicted when his fighter burst into flames after hitting the ground.

No. 457 Sqn was the last to attack, led by Caldwell himself, but its 7,000ft height advantage also led to an exceptionally high attack speed. This again meant very difficult and fleeting shots, which, when combined with cannon failures, resulted in only two pilots claiming hits on the bombers. It was thought that the exceptionally long period No. 1 Fighter Wing had spent at high altitude prior to intercepting the enemy aircraft had contributed to the widespread gun problems experienced on 30 June.

Despite these attacks from above, the 'Betty' pilots from the 753rd Kokutai successfully completed their bombing runs on Fenton – a testament to their discipline and ability. Furthermore, the bombing was deadly accurate and inflicted notable damage on the 380th BG, including the destruction of three B-24s.

By then, many of the No. 1 Fighter Wing pilots were beginning to run out of oxygen and had to return to base. Despite this, a handful of them stalked the bombers on their way out, including Caldwell and Gibbs, with the latter feeling the effects of hypoxia. Both pilots made attack runs against bombers, but were reduced to using only their 0.303-in. machine guns, because of cannon failures.

Overall, it was another frustrating day for the Spitfire pilots, with seven fighters lost (three to mechanical failures) and two pilots killed. No enemy aircraft were downed in return. However, nine 'Bettys' had suffered some damage, and three crewmen were killed. The failure to bring a single bomber

FPO1c Kurakazu Goto was a newly trained pilot when he joined the 202nd Kokutai in late 1942, although he quickly claimed his first victory when he downed a B-24 in February 1943. Goto flew his first mission over Darwin the following month. He was credited with a second Liberator destroyed and three RAAF Beaufighters probably destroyed in May, and participated in two more Darwin missions the following month. On 7 September, Goto claimed three Spitfires shot down and a fourth as a probable during yet another attack on Darwin, taking his tally to eight victories. He failed to return from a mission over Merauke, in central Dutch New Guinea, 48 hours later. (Tony Holmes Collection)

down, despite pilots having hit a number of them multiple times, reflected attacks made with machine guns only. The rifle-calibre 0.303-in. weapons patently lacked the destructive power required to inflict fatal damage on a 'Betty'. With a reliable cannon armament, it could have been a different story.

Perhaps recognising the threat posed by the B-24 heavy bombers of the 380th BG to its bases in the NEI, the IJNAF mounted a follow-up Fenton raid on 6 July 1943. The attacking force comprised 21 'Bettys' from the 753rd Kokutai escorted by 26 A6M2s, led by Lt Toshio Shiozuru, from the 202nd Kokutai. The incoming raid was detected at 1037 hrs, and minutes later 33 Spitfires were airborne (albeit again without belly tanks – replacement stock had still not arrived). With Caldwell leading, a wing rendezvous was made over Sattler. The track of the raiders was even more southerly than during the 30 June attack, leaving little doubt as to the intended target. The enemy aircraft climbed to 20,000ft on crossing the coast, by which point No. 1 Fighter Wing was just 20 miles away at an altitude of 32,000ft. Fighter control ordered a direct interception, and 'Tally Ho' was quickly called over the radio as visual contact was made via the sun glinting on the bomber canopies.

Caldwell manoeuvred the wing into an up-sun position, flying parallel to the enemy, although by now the bombers had climbed to 27,000ft. He then told his pilots to make a pincer attack just as he had attempted a week earlier. In order to do this, No. 54 Sqn had to fly over the enemy so as to be ready to attack from the opposite side of the IJNAF formation. Following some confusion within No. 452 Sqn as to what target its pilots were to go after, one section was ordered to take on the fighters while another went for the bombers. On this day Caldwell was flying with No. 457 Sqn, which he initially kept above the Japanese formation in reserve. Meanwhile, the usual mechanical failures that plagued No. 1 Fighter Wing throughout 1943 had reduced its strength by three aircraft to 30.

Flt Lt Ted Hall led a section of No. 452 Sqn Spitfires against a group of nine Zero-sens. However, the latter were flying tight defensive turns – an effective tactic to employ against the fast-diving Spitfires. Although no hits were made on the enemy aircraft, Hall's section had at least drawn nine of the escorts away from the bombers. The squadron's second section was led by Flt Lt Paul St John Makin, who, after intending to make a frontal attack on the 'Bettys', at the last moment went after a detached section of Zero-sens. In the subsequent combat, a number of A6M2s managed to get on the tail of some of the No. 452 Sqn Spitfires, resulting in Flg Off Clive Lloyd being forced to bail out of his badly shot up aircraft. Two more Spitfires from the unit were lost to CSU failures, while Flt Sgt Jeff King ran out of oxygen and passed out due to hypoxia. He regained consciousness in a high-speed dive and was fortunate to return safely to base. Five more squadron aircraft had cannon stoppages.

Meanwhile, Sqn Ldr Bill Gibbs led No. 54 Sqn in a frontal attack against the bombers. He once again experienced cannon failure, although he still claimed hits on the lead bomber with his machine guns. Several other pilots also observed hits on 'Bettys', with some showing signs of damage and one dropping out of formation altogether. Flt Sgt J. M. Wickman made two attacking runs against this straggler, but

Lt Sada-o Yamaguchi flew a number of missions over northern Australia in 1942–43, and made several victory claims against No. 1 Fighter Wing Spitfires prior to being posted back to Japan in July. Yamaguchi claimed his first two (of 12) victories over the NEI on 3 February 1942. Seeing action over Guadalcanal from Rabaul between September and November that same year, Yamaguchi survived an emergency landing on the north coast of Guadalcanal after being shot down by US fighters– he was rescued by friendly forces and returned to Rabaul. In October 1943 he was posted to the Rabaul-based 204th Kokutai as a buntaicho and fought with the unit (claiming five victories) until it was withdrawn to Truk in late January 1944. Returning to Japan in May and joining the Yokosuka Kokutai, Yamaguchi was assigned to the Hachiman Force the following month and sent to Iwo Jima to participate in the *A-Go* offensive. Intercepting US Navy carrier aircraft over the Mariana Islands on several occasions, he was killed on 4 July. (Tony Holmes Collection)

A relaxed Flt Lt Teddy Hall prepares for a sortie from Darwin in June 1943. A veteran of combat on the Channel Front with No. 129 Sqn in 1942 (during which time he had claimed a share in the destruction of an He 59 floatplane and probably destroyed an He 115 floatplane, both off Cherbourg on 18 August), Hall had been credited with damaging 'Hamps' during the 15 March and 2 May raids. He was subsequently credited with the destruction of a 'Zeke' on 30 June and a 'Hamp' on 6 July. All of Hall's claims in 1943 came in Spitfire VC BS186/QY-L. (Andrew Thomas Collection)

was hit from behind by a Zero-sen and forced to bail out of his crippled machine.

After these two attacks had gone in, Caldwell ordered two of No. 457 Sqn's sections to attack when the enemy formation was 20 miles from Fenton. He remained above in reserve with a third section of three aircraft. Experiencing their fair share of cannon failures, the two sections dived through a hornet's nest of A6M2s as they made high-speed runs on the bombers. Blue Section, reduced to three aircraft after one pilot dropped out due to radio failure, made the mistake of turning around for a repeat attack right under the noses of the Zero-sens. The victims of what appears to have been a perfect bounce, Flg Off F. D. Hamilton and Plt Offs N. Robinson and F. R. J. McDowell were all killed in their cockpits, having almost certainly fallen victim to close-range cannon fire.

As the bombers approached Fenton, various observers noticed the unusually ragged nature of the 'Betty' formation – five bombers were lagging behind. Unlike previous raids, on this occasion the Spitfires had inflicted some damage on the aircraft prior to bomb release. However, this appeared to have only a limited effect on the 753rd Kokutai as the lead bombardier once again dropped with admirable precision from high altitude. One B-24 was destroyed and a large fuel dump went up in flames. Their ordnance gone, the bombers now wheeled around and headed for home.

Caldwell, whose section of three aircraft was still up above the IJNAF formation in reserve, was in one of the few Spitfire VCs equipped with drop tanks that day. The fighters flown by his wingmen lacked tanks, however, and their available fuel was now getting precariously low. Hence, both pilots dived down to attack the bombers without their leader, although they were blocked by Zero-sens that were maintaining a keen lookout. Other individual Spitfire pilots were able to make attacks on the bombers as they headed north for the coast, although they were hampered by fuel and oxygen limitations. There was also the usual share of CSU problems that contributed to the loss of three more aircraft. Caldwell himself finally attacked while the enemy formation was re-crossing the coast. After targeting a bomber, he found three Zero-sens on his tail and broke off the engagement.

One 'Betty' did indeed crash, with the loss of its eight-man crew. The wreckage was found in a swamp near Welltree Station, and the bodies of the crew and parts of the bomber were recovered. Two other bombers crashed upon their return to Timor, presumably as a result of combat damage.

On 30 June and 6 July, the IJNAF had confirmed its ability to strike deep at the 380th BG's Fenton base. Unlike smaller aircraft, four-engined heavy bombers such as the B-24 were appreciably more difficult to disperse protectively and camouflage. While Allied air commanders waited nervously for follow-up strikes, the Japanese almost certainly missed the opportunity to launch a low-level Zero-sen strike on the base that could have produced devastating results.

Indeed, despite increasing attrition in New Guinea and Guadalcanal, the IJNAF had managed to maintain air strength in the NEI that was not greatly diminished from that with which it had started 1943. On 15 July the 753rd Kokutai had 39 'Bettys' on strength, of which 25 were operational. The 202nd Kokutai could muster 63 A6M2s, although only 37 were operational, as well as nine A6M3s (with ten more in the process of being delivered). The 202nd was also still assigned four C5M2 'Babs' (two operational), although these had not flown reconnaissance missions over Australia since March. Such sorties were now exclusively being undertaken by IJAAF 'Dinahs' of the 70th DCS. In a rare example of the IJAAF and the IJNAF operating the same type of aircraft,

WO Kiyoshi Ito poses with his A6M3 at Koepang prior to flying a long-range mission to northern Australia in 1943. He had joined the 3rd Kokutai in November 1941 after completing his flying training, and due to his lack of combat experience (many of the pilots then serving with the unit had more than a thousand hours in fighters) Ito had to wait until 4 April 1942 to make his first victory claim – a P-40 over Darwin. From then until he was sent to Rabaul in September of that same year, Ito steadily added to his tally of aerial successes. Following two months of bitter fighting over Guadalcanal, he returned to Kendari and resumed flying missions over northern Australia between March and September 1943. By the time Ito was sent back to Japan at the end of the year to serve out the rest of the war as an instructor, he had participated in 30 aerial engagements and claimed 18 aircraft shot down and 14 damaged. (Tony Holmes Collection)

the 202nd Kokutai had also received two Ki-46-IIs of its own.

The 'Dinah' missions had continued to be flown on a regular basis, and these proved frustrating for No. 1 Fighter Wing, which had not managed any successful interceptions since March. Its luck changed on the morning of 18 July when the CO of No. 457 Sqn, Sqn Ldr Ken James, shot down a 'Dinah' that was attempting to photograph Fenton airfield. Among the two crew killed was the CO of the 70th DCS, Capt Sunji Sasaki. This loss was deeply felt by the IJAAF, as Sasaki was a veteran of many successful flights over Australia.

On the night of 13 August, 12 'Bettys' from the 753rd Kokutai returned to bomb Darwin, Fenton and a number of other locations. This was a reversion to the tactics of late 1942, and unescorted night bombing would be the norm for the next few months. However, this virtually took the form of nuisance raids, as hardly any damage of significance was inflicted. It seems that pressures from New Guinea and elsewhere (including the need to defend their own bases from B-24 raids) meant that both the 753rd and the 202nd Kokutais were no longer available to mount maximum effort daylight raids that had characterised much of 1943.

Just four days later, on 17 August, a very determined reconnaissance effort appeared to be underway as five 'Dinahs' from the 70th DCS were detected by radar. Within a period of just 30 minutes three of them had been downed by No. 1 Fighter Wing. One of the Ki-46s had been carrying a doll that was intended to be dropped over Fenton in memory of Capt Sasaki. The action was not over for the day, however, as that afternoon Wg Cdr Caldwell shared in the destruction of one of the 202nd Kokutai's Ki-46s. This was a major victory for No. 1 Fighter Wing, and clear evidence that its interception skills had improved.

The Japanese responded with an escorted reconnaissance on 7 September, with two 'Dinahs' from the 70th DCS being accompanied by a strong force of 36 Zero-sens from the 202nd Kokutai – the fighters were led by Lt Cdr Minoru Suzuki. The incoming formation was detected well out to sea at 0837 hrs, and a full wing rendezvous was made over Sattler at 25,000ft. Nos. 54 and 457 Sqns contributed 13 aircraft each, while No. 452 Sqn sent ten aloft. On this day the wing was

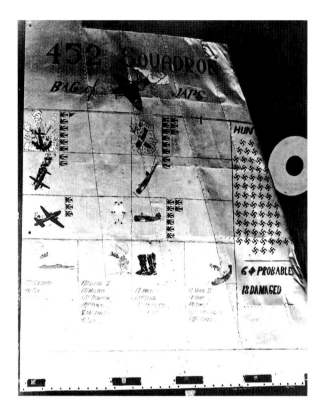

The scoreboard (most likely part of a 'Betty' or 'Dinah'), christened *BAG of JAPS*, used by No. 452 Sqn. Alongside eight-and-a-half bombers and 11 fighters destroyed, it also includes more than 50 claims made against the Luftwaffe in 1941–42. It was not until the 1970s that a detailed analysis of IJNAF and IJAAF records revealed that claims by No. 1 Fighter Wing were around three times actual Japanese losses in 1943. The bottom line of the scoreboard features a tally of which pilots had bailed out over the water, over the land, force-landed and walked back to base, and crash-landed on the airfield. (Andrew Thomas Collection)

commanded by No. 54 Sqn's Flt Lt Bob Foster, as Caldwell was due to be posted to an OTU. However, communications largely failed among the Spitfire pilots, as one radio had been left on in 'transmit' mode. In the absence of a good radio network, co-ordination suffered. Instead, most of the wing followed Foster in a climb towards the last reported position of the enemy. In doing so, the wing climbed right up towards the Zero-sens, thus setting up a perfect bounce for the IJNAF fighters.

In the subsequent combat, the Japanese pilots attacked with the benefit of height out of the sun. Several Spitfire pilots duly found themselves under attack with little warning. Indeed, many were probably looking out for the customary 'Betty' formation and had missed the Zero-sens altogether – they were much harder to spot. Given this disadvantage, it is not surprising that three Spitfires (including the aircraft flown by No. 452 Sqn CO Sqn Ldr Ron MacDonald, who bailed out wounded) were shot down and Flg Off W. T. Hinds killed. On this occasion the No. 1 Fighter Wing pilots mounted a number of spirited counter-attacks and believed that they had shot down five Zero-sens. However, only one A6M2 loss can be confirmed, which resulted in the death of FPO1c Yoshio Terai (who was a 1942 flying school graduate – further evidence that like No. 1 Fighter Wing, the 202nd Kokutai now had its own share of fairly inexperienced pilots).

Despite the losses suffered on 7 September, the Spitfire pilots were encouraged by the appearance of a large Zero-sen formation in daylight over Darwin, and expected further action to follow. However, this engagement would be the last time that Spitfires and A6Ms clashed over the skies of northern Australia. The very last Zero-sen mission over Australia occurred on 27 September when just four A6M2s from the 202nd Kokutai escorted an IJAAF force of 21 Ki-48s from the 75th Sentai against Drysdale airfield and the nearby Kalumburu Mission of the Benedictine Order in Western Australia.

Otherwise, the only aerial activity before the end of 1943 was the occasional reconnaissance mission and night raid. The very last attack took place in the early hours of 11 November when eight 'Bettys' from the 753rd Kokutai bombed a variety of targets. Spitfires flying as nightfighters were vectored towards the aircraft, and Flg Off Jack Smithson of No. 457 Sqn was able to spot the bombers with the aid of a searchlight. Approaching from dead astern at 20,000ft, Smithson was fortunate enough to have cannons that worked as intended and his quarry burst into flames and dived to the ground. Among the crew killed were two very senior 753rd Kokutai officers in the form of hikotaicho Cdr Michio Hori and buntaicho Lt Takeharu Fujiwara. Their loss was a major blow to the unit, and further Darwin missions were immediately cancelled. The downing of this 'Betty' marked the end of the air campaign over Darwin in 1943.

STATISTICS AND ANALYSIS

The statistics in respect to confirmed fighter losses during the aerial engagements over Darwin in 1943 indicate a resounding victory for the Japanese – 38 Spitfires destroyed versus just six Japanese fighters (five Zero-sens and a single 'Oscar'). However, these figures are skewed by the many Spitfire losses caused by mechanical failures or fuel shortages. Also, available Japanese records are not as detailed as Allied ones, and it is possible that some of the damaged Zero-sens which returned to Timor were subsequently written off. These would need to be added to known Japanese losses for a proper accounting of the campaign to be made.

A total of 15 No. 1 Fighter Wing pilots lost their lives in combat during 1943, while Japanese losses totalled just six fighter pilots. Even allowing for the fact that not all of the No. 1 Fighter Wing losses were directly attributable to the Zero-sens, it is difficult not to conclude that the Japanese had the upper hand in these aerial battles. However, it is unfair to judge No. 1 Fighter Wing purely in terms of fighter-versus-fighter combat, as its primary role was to shoot down bombers. Also, when the losses of Japanese bomber and reconnaissance aircraft are included in the victory count, No. 1 Fighter Wing had a kill-to-loss ratio of approximating one-to-one – a figure achieved by many other World War II fighter units in a variety of theatres.

The obvious problem when analysing No. 1 Fighter Wing's performance is that the unit's Spitfire VCs were plagued by serious technical issues (specifically the serviceability of its CSUs and cannon) throughout 1943. It is difficult to quantify how the wing would have fared in the absence of these problems. Possibly, the outcome of the fighter-versus-fighter combat might not have been greatly different, but it is highly

Sqn Ldr Bill Gibbs indicates to his groundcrew to remove the wheel chocks from BS164/DL-K, as he is ready to taxi out at RAAF Base Darwin. His aircraft carries whiskey nips for all six of his victory claims (five and one shared destroyed), plus a solitary glass for the 'Zeke' credited to Flt Lt Robin Norwood on 15 March. BS164 was involved in all of these successes. (Peter R. Arnold Collection)

likely that more 'Bettys' would have been lost to properly functioning Hispano cannon.

Certainly, the Zero-sen pilots were far better organised and disciplined when it came to flying together in mutually supporting formations. On the odd occasion when a Spitfire pilot thought he was tackling a lone A6M2, typically, he would soon find himself quickly coming under attack from other IJNAF fighters. This reflected the greater experience of the 202nd Kokutai pilots, and the fact that many of these individuals had been flying together in continuous combat operations since late 1941.

Conversely, No. 1 Fighter Wing had commenced operations in 1943 with a substantial cadre of newly trained aviators, and it took time for combat experience to filter through the unit as a whole. A lack of operational awareness manifested itself in various ways, including, for example, failing to maintain a proper lookout for the enemy. The Spitfire pilots repeatedly proved deficient in this respect, being overly reliant on radio warnings – from fellow pilots and ground controllers – instead. Furthermore, on numerous occasions Spitfire pilots were dismissive of Zero-sens appearing to 'show-off' with aerobatic manoeuvres prior to engaging them in combat. They seemingly failed to have understood that the Japanese pilots were simply banking steeply or rolling in order to achieve a better lookout over as much of the sky as possible.

In the Darwin environment, 'Big Wing' ('Balbo') tactics clearly failed. Excessive fuel was used in forming up the wing, and the centralised command and control robbed squadron leaders of the opportunity to use their initiative and attack when conditions were favourable. Also, the 'Big Wing' formation was easily seen by the Japanese, who could then take defensive precautions against it.

In strategic terms, No. 1 Fighter Wing was effective in opposing every daylight raid with a major formation of fighters. During the campaign the Japanese believed, through their own excessive claiming, that they were inflicting such losses on the Spitfires as to seriously compromise the air defence of Darwin. Yet this was never the case, and the wing kept rising in numbers that must have continually surprised the IJNAF.

From a Japanese perspective, they succeeded in their goal of launching regular raids against Darwin during 1943 (every one of which saw despatched 'Betty' bombers defended effectively by their Zero-sen escorts). Their initial attacks against Fenton threatened to do real damage to the newly arrived 380th BG, but just as soon as these began the whole Japanese air campaign petered out. Certainly, the airmanship displayed by the pilots of the 202nd Kokutai pilots was extremely impressive, as was the reliability of their Zero-sens during such long-range missions. However, towards the end of the campaign there were signs that the hard-won experience was starting to pay dividends within No. 1 Fighter Wing, and if another aerial campaign against northern Australia had materialised during the dry season of 1944, the results of the fighter-versus-fighter combats would probably have been much more even.

AFTERMATH

Following the end of the 1943 Darwin campaign, large-scale aerial battles never resumed over northern Australia. In April 1944 the surviving Spitfire VCs began to be replaced by the vastly superior Spitfire VIII. The following month Nos. 54 and 457 Sqns detached to Exmouth Gulf, in Western Australia. Here, they covered the refuelling of a group of Allied warships undertaking offensive operations in the Indian Ocean, but there was no enemy interference.

At this time No. 1 Fighter Wing was reorganised, with No. 54 Sqn being joined by newly formed RAF units Nos. 548 and 549 Sqns. Flying Spitfire VIIIs, these squadrons guarded the Darwin area until early 1945. However, they faced only occasional

The tropical background to No. 452 Sqn's dispersal at Balikpapan in July 1945 belies the harsh conditions the units of No. 80 Fighter Wing endured while operating their Spitfire VIIIs in support of 'mopping-up' operations during the campaign to retake the NEI. (Andrew Thomas Collection)

Japanese reconnaissance flights, and as Australian Spitfire historian Stewart Wilson has written:

> Unserviceability was high, flying hours and combat opportunities (and therefore morale) were low, and it was with a whimper rather than a bang that meaningful Spitfire operations in northern Australia ended.

Meanwhile, both Nos. 452 and 457 Sqns had been allocated to the RAAF's 1st Tactical Air Force, which it was hoped would see action in the island-hopping campaign moving north through the Philippines. Together with No. 79 Sqn, which had operated Spitfire VCs in New Guinea from mid-May 1943, these units were newly designated as No. 80 Fighter Wing. After the capture of Morotai Island, located midway between New Guinea and the Philippines, the wing moved there in late 1944 with its Spitfire VIIIs in preparation for the final offensives against Japan.

However, it was soon clear that there would be sparse opportunity for aerial combat. Instead, No. 80 Fighter Wing was relegated to assisting with 'mopping-up' operations over nearby islands of the NEI. Many pilots viewed these close-support missions in tropical conditions as excessively risky and unnecessary, and several senior officers, including now-Gp Capt Clive Caldwell, resigned their commissions in an unfortunate series of events that became known as the 'Morotai Mutiny'.

The wing's final operations occurred in mid-1945, when Nos. 452 and 457 Sqns moved to Borneo in support of the Allied landings there. On 24 July, in one of the few aerial combats to take place at this time, No. 452 Sqn's Flg Off J. C. King shot down an IJAAF 'Helen' bomber. This proved to be the final victory achieved by the RAAF in World War II, and also the last of countless wartime kills credited to Spitfires worldwide.

In contrast, many of No. 1 Fighter Wing's former adversaries went on to see plenty of hard fighting during the final two years of the war. Towards the end of 1943, about half of the pilots assigned to the 202nd Kokutai were detached for service from Rabaul. Others remained at scattered locations throughout the NEI, where their duties included nightfighter defence with J1N1 'Irvings'.

In March 1944 the 202nd Kokutai moved to the Central Pacific, and in another IJNAF reorganisation it became composed of two new units, Sento 301st and 603rd Hikotais. Both of these units saw combat flying Zero-sens against American heavy bombers and carrier air groups. Lt Cdr Minoru Suzuki, who had led the 202nd Kokutai throughout most of the 1943 Darwin campaign, remained in command until March 1944. Four months later, in July 1944, both the 202nd Kokutai and 603rd Hikotai were disbanded. At the same time the 301st Hikotai became part of the 201st Kokutai and participated in the defence of the Philippines. Further reorganisations followed, and during 1945 the 301st Hikotai saw action over Okinawa and Japan through to the end of the war.

Spitfire VC BR545 emerges from its watery grave in the Prince Regent River, near Derby, in Western Australia, on 28 November 1987. Formerly No. 54 Sqn's 'DL-E', it had served with the unit in the defence of Darwin from mid-November 1942 to 22 December 1943. On the latter date, it was being ferried from Nightcliff, near Darwin, to Drysdale mission field in Western Australia by Flt Lt D. W. Gray when he became lost en route. Running low on fuel, he force-landed on tidal mud flats – Gray noted in his logbook 'crashed in swamp, four days and nights in dinghy'. He was eventually rescued by a Walrus flying boat on Christmas Day, 1943. BR545 remained in the mudflats until November 1987, when a 14-man RAAF team recovered it for preservation by the RAAF Museum at RAAF Base Point Cook, Victoria. Although the fighter appeared to be substantially intact when in situ on the mudflats, it was found to be badly corroded. The recovered airframe has never been put on public display. (Peter R. Arnold Collection)

FURTHER READING

BOOKS

Alexander, Kristen, *Clive Caldwell Air Ace* (Allen & Unwin, 2006)

Alford, Bob, *Darwin's Air War 1942–1945* (Aviation Historical Society of the Northern Territory, 2011)

Alford, Bob, *Japanese Air Forces over the NWA 1942–1945* (Robert N. Alford, 2011)

Claringbould, Michael, *Spitfire Sunday* (*Flightpath* magazine, 2008)

Claringbould, Michael and Ruffato, Luca, *Eagles of the Southern Sky – The Tainan Air Group in World War II, Volume One: New Guinea* (Tainan Research and Publishing, 2012)

Cooper, Anthony, *Darwin Spitfires* (University of New South Wales Press Ltd, 2011)

Gillison, Douglas, *Royal Australian Air Force 1939–1942, Australia in the War of 1939–1945, Series Three Air, Volume I* (Australian War Memorial, 1962)

Grant, Jim, *Spitfires Over Darwin 1943* (TechWrite Solutions, 1995 (reprinted 2003))

Hata, Ikuhiko, Izawa, Yashuo and Shores, Christopher, *Japanese Naval Air Force Fighter Units and their Aces 1932–1945* (Grub Street, 2011)

Lewis, Tom, *The Empire Strikes South – Japan's Air War Against Northern Australia 1942–45* (Avonmore Books, 2017)

Lewis, Tom and Ingman, Peter, *Zero Hour in Broome* (Avonmore Books, 2010)

Murphy, Ralph and Gay, *The Making of a Spitfire Pilot – The Battle of Britain to the Timor Sea – The War Diaries of R. K. C. Norwood 1940–46* (Ralph Murphy, 2016)

Odgers, George, *Air War Against Japan 1943–1945, Australia in the War of 1939–1945, Series Three Air, Volume III* (Australian War Memorial, 1957)

Shores, Christopher, *Those Other Eagles* (Grub Street, 2004)

Shores, Christopher and Cull, Brian, with Izawa, Yashuo, *Bloody Shambles Volume 1 – The Drift to War to the Fall of Singapore* (Grub Street, 1992)

Shores, Christopher and Cull, Brian, with Izawa, Yashuo, *Bloody Shambles Volume 2 – The Defence of Sumatra to the Fall of Burma* (Grub Street, 1993)

Shores, Christopher and Williams, Clive, *Aces High* (Grub Street, 1994)

Thomas, Andrew, *Osprey Aircraft of the Aces 87 – Spitfire Aces of Burma and the Pacific* (Osprey Publishing, 2009)

Watson, Jeffrey, *Killer Caldwell – Australia's Greatest Fighter Pilot* (Hodder, 2005)

Wilson, Stewart, *Spitfire, Mustang and Kittyhawk in Australian Service* (Aerospace Publications, 1988)

WEBSITES

adf-gallery.com.au (ADF Serials site)

darwinspitfires.com (addendum site to *Darwin Spitfires* book by Anthony Cooper)

INDEX

Note: page locators in **bold** refer to illustrations, captions and plates.

A6M2 Zero-sen fighter aeroplane (Japan) 2, 4, 5, 7, 8, **8**, 10, 12, **13**, **14**, 16, 17, **18**, 19, **20**, **23**, 25, **28**, 28–29, **30**, 35, **36**, 37, **38**, 39, 40–41, **41**, 46–47, **50–52**, 52–53, 54, 55, 57, **63**, **66**, 66–68, **67**, **68**, **69**, 71, 72, 74, 75
aces 2, 5, 19, 33, 34, **34**, **40**, **44–45**, 46, 48, **48**, **53**, 55, **60**, **61**, **64**, 73, **73**
Aioi, Lt Takahide **45**, 48, 52, **52**
aircraft 4, 5, 10, 12, 32, 38
    A5M 'Claude' fighter aeroplane (Japan) 35, **45**
    A6M3 Zero 'Hamp' fighter aeroplane (Japan) 13–16, **15**, **20**, 23, 28, **60**, 62, 72, **72**
    B-24 Liberator bomber aeroplane (US) 27, **28**, 38, 39, 63, 70, **70**, 71, 72
    Beaufighter fighter aeroplane (UK) 29, 52, 62
    C5M 'Babs' reconnaissance aeroplane (Japan) **25**, 28, 30, 36, 38, 39, **40**, 73
    G4M 'Betty' bomber aeroplane (Japan) 2, 7, 8, 24, **25**, 27, **28**, 30, 38, 39, 40, 49, 54, 55, 57, 58, **58**, 60, **60**, 62, 63, 66, **66**, 68, 70, 71, 72, 73, 74, 76
    Hudson bomber aeroplane (UK) 31, 37, 62
    Ki-43 'Oscar' fighter aeroplane (Japan) 5, 63, 64, 65, 66
    Ki-46 'Dinah' reconnaissance aeroplane (Japan) 8, 30, **49**, 52, 54, 57, 63, 66, 68, 73
    Ki-48 'Lily' bomber aeroplane (Japan) 8, 63, 65, 74
    Ki-49 'Helen' bomber aeroplane (Japan) 63, 64, 65, 66, 78
    P-40E Warhawk fighter aeroplane (US) 6, 20, 24, 25, 27, **27**, 30, 32, 37, 38, 40, 41, **45**, 46, 49, 73
    RoCAF I-15/I-16 fighter aeroplanes (China) 7, 35, **45**
    Spitfire Mk V fighter aeroplane (UK) 5, 12
    Spitfire Mk VB fighter aeroplane (UK) 33, **33**, 42
    Spitfire Mk VC tropicals 12–13, 15–16
    Spitfire Mk VIII fighter aeroplane (UK) 5, 77, **77**, 78
Allied strategy 24, 27, **41**, 56, 57–58, 64, 65, 66, 68, **68**, **69**, 70, 71, 72, 76
armoured protection **16**
Arnold, Gen Henry 'Hap' 15
Australian defence plans 31–32

'Balbo' tactics 7, 42, 54, 57, 61, 64, 66, 76
Battle of Britain, the 10, 32–33, **44**
Battle of the Java Sea, the 38
Broome mission, the **38**, 38–39, 47
Brothers, Sqn Ldr Pete 34

Caldwell, Wg Cdr Clive 2, 5, 7, 34, 42–43, **45**, **49**, 52, **52**, 53, 54, 56, 57–58, 61, 64, 66, **66**, 68, **68**, 70, 71, 72, 73, 74, 78
camouflage 25, **25**, **30**, 65, **68**
cannon failure 53, 56, 60, 65, 70, 72, 75
Churchill, Winston 7, 32, **55**
cockpits **16**, **21**, **44**, **59**, **67**
combat ceilings 16, **18**
Coomalie Creek raid 8, **45**, 52, **52**, 53
Cooper, Anthony 32, 56
Cresswell, Sqn Ldr Dick 27–28
CSU failures 22, 23, 58, 61, 62, 65, 68, 71, 72, 75

Darwin dry season campaign (1943), the 5, 7, 8, 12, 39–41, **44**, 49–74, **50–52**, 76
Darwin raid by the IJAAF 63–66, **68**
Darwin Spitfires (book) 32
Davao deployment, the 36–37
design and development 9–16, **15**, 21, 23
drop tanks **18**, 61, **68**, 72

EATS (Empire Air Training Scheme) 31, 33, 34
elliptical wings 9, **9**, 10

engines 10, 12, 16, **18**, **23**, **36**
Fenton raids 2,8, 68, 70, 71–72, 76
fighter-*versus*-fighter combat 46–47, **50–52**, 53, 55, 58–60, 62, 66–68, **69**, 71, 74, 75–76
Finucane, Flt Lt Brendan 'Paddy' 33, **34**
formation tactics **41**, 42, 46–47, 53, 56, 64, 68, 72, 76
'Fortress Singapore' surrender 31, 32
Foster, Flt Lt R.W. 'Bob' **5**, 33, **42**, 43, 74
fuel exhaustion 60, 61
fuselage codes **9**, **12**, **66**

Gibbs, Sqn Ldr Eric 'Bill' **5**, 33, 52, **52**, 53, 66, 68, 70, **76**
Goldsmith, Flg Off Tim 55, 60, **60**
Guadalcanal campaign, the 7, 28, 30, 35, 41, 46, 47, **71**
gun heater problems 21–22, **22**

Hall, Flt Lt Ted 54, 71, **72**
Hashiguchi, FPO 1c Yoshiro **62**, **63**

IJAAF (Imperial Japanese Army Air Force) 5, 7, 8, 10, 63, 64, **68**, 73
    70th DCS (Dokuritsu Hiko Chutai) 30, 73
IJN carrier raid on Darwin, February 1942 24
IJNAF (Imperial Japanese Navy Air Force) 5, 10, 24, **28**, **43**, 47-48, 70, 71, 72
    12th Kokutai 35, 38, **45**
    202nd (3rd) Kokutai 5, 7, 8, **8**, 16, 23, 25, **25**, 28, **28**, 29, 30, 35–39, **37**, **38**, **40**, 41, **45**, 47, 48, 52, 54, 56, 57, 60, 61, 62, **62**, 63, 66, 68, 71, 73, **73**, 74, 76, 78
    753rd (Takao) Kokutai 2, 24, **25**, **28**, 30, 39, 40, 41, 49, 54, 57, 58, 63, 66, 68, 70, 71, 72, 73, 74
    Tainan Kokutai **13**, 15, 35, 38, 47

Japanese air strength 28–30, 72–73
Japanese strategy 5–6, 24, 27, 28, **28**, 29, 30, 36–39, **41**, **43**, 46–47, 73, 76

Kendari airfield 29, 37
KNIL-ML (Royal Netherlands East Indies Army Air Force) 36, 37

losses 2, 5, 27, 34, 35, 36, 37–38, 39, 40–41, 47, **53**, 55, 56, 60, 61, 62, 63, 65, 70, 71, 72, 73, 74, 75
Luftwaffe, the 7, 34, **43**, **74**
Luzon escort raid 36, **36**, 37

Malta theatre, the 43–46
manoeuvrability 15, **15**, 16, 17, 19, 53, **60**, 62, 76
map of northern Australia and the NEI **26–27**
Mawer, Flg Off Al 2, **30**, **53**, 55, **55**, 65
medals and honours 33, 34, **60**
Menado invasion, the 37
Milingimbi Island airstrip attack 8, 61–63, **63**, 64
Mitchell, Reginald J. 9
'Morotai Mutiny', the 78
museum exhibits **10**, 56, **78**

NEI (Netherlands East Indies) 5, 7, 24, **26–27**, 27, 30, 36–37, **41**, 57, **61**, **71**, **77**, 78
Norwood, Flt Lt Robin **5**, **9**, **12**, 33, **42**, **44**, **76**

Operation *I-Go* (April 1943) 57

performance 9, **9**, 12, 13, **15**, 15–16, 17, **18**, 53
pilot experience 5, 31, 33–35, 41, **44–45**, 46, 47–48, **48**, **49**, **73**, 76
propeller jamming 22–23
prototypes 9–10

RAAF (Royal Australian Air Force) 13, 24, 25, 61–62
    No. 1 Fighter Wing 5, 7, 8, 21, **21**, 22, 23, 27, 28, **29**, 31, 32, 34, **41**, **42**, 42–46, 47, 48, 49, 52, **55**, 56, 61, 64, 75, 76
    No. 31 Sqn 29, 52
    No. 44 (Radar) wing 27, **29**
    No. 54 Sqn (RAF) 2, **4**, 5, **5**, 7, 8, **9**, **12**, **21**, **25**, 30, 32, 33, **44**, **46**, **52**, **53**, **53**, 54–55, **55**, 57, 58–60, 64, 65, 66, 62, 8–70, 71, 73–74, 77
    No. 75 Sqn 32
    No. 76 Sqn 32, 49
    No. 77 Sqn 27–28, 32, 49
    No. 79 Sqn 5, **10**
    No. 452 Sqn 5, 7, 22–23, 32, **32–33**, 33, 34, **34**, 49, **49**, **53**, 54, **54**, 57, 58, 64, 65, **65**, 66, 71, 73, 74, **74**, 77, 78
    No. 457 Sqn 5, 7, 8, 32, 34, 49, **49**, 52, 54, 56, 57, 58, 60, 62, 64, 68–70, 72, 73, 74, 77, 78
radar networks 27, **29**, 74
radio systems 47, 64, 76
RAF, the 5, 32–33, 34, **44**, 54, 77-78
range 17, **18**, 35
reconnaissance 30, **30**, 38, **49**, 53–54, 57, 63, 68, 73–74, 78
RoCAF (Republic of China Air Force), the 7, 35, **45**

scoreboards **55**, 57, **68**, **74**, 76
Second Sino-Japanese War, the 35, 38, **45**
shotai fighter formation 6, **28**, **43**, 46, 62
Spitfire Mk VC fighter aeroplane (UK) 2, 5, 6, 7, **9**, **11**, 12, 13, 16, 17, 20–21, **22**, 30, 32, **43**, **44**, 46, **50–52**, 52, 53, **54**, 55, 56, 58–60, **59**, 61, 62–63, **63**, 66–68, **69**, 70, **72**, 75, 77, **78**
    BS164 **68**, **76**
    BS295 **50–52**, **66**
    EE853 **10**, **16**
    LZ846 **11–12**
Strauss, Capt Allison W. 25
Stuart Highway dispersed airfields 24–25, **29**, **30**
Sugi-o, WO Shigeo 48, **48**
Suzuki, Lt Cdr Minoru 57, **57**, **62**, 78

TAIU-SWPA 15
technical problems 21–23, **22**, 53, 56, 58, 61, 62, 64, 65, 68, 70, 71, 72, 75
technical specifications **18**
testing 13, 15–16
Thorold-Smith, Sqn Ldr Ray 2, 33, **34**, **42**, 54, 55, 56, 58
training 31, 33, 34, 35, 42, 43, **44**, **45**, 46, 47, 54
Truscott, Flt Lt Keith 'Bluey' 33, **34**

undercarriages 16, **43**
USAAC, the 7, 36, 38
USAAF, the
    49th FG 5–6, 7, 24, 25, 27, **27**, 40, 46
    319th BS 27
    380th BG 63, 68, 70, 71, 72, 76

Vokes filter 12–13

Walters, Gp Capt 52, 53
Watson, Flt Sgt Rex 65
weaponry 12, 29
    Browning 0.303-in. machine gun (UK) 9, **10**, 12, 18, **22**, 70, 71
    Browning M2 0.50 cal machine gun (US) **27**
    Hispano Mk II cannon (UK) 18, 20, **20**, 21, **21**, **22**, **69**, 76
    Type 97 7.7mm machine gun (Japan) 18, **19**, **20**, 53, 55–56, 60
    Type 99-1 20mm cannon (Japan) 10, 12, 18, **19**, 19–20, **20**, **21**, 55–56, 60, 63
Wilson, Stewart 32

Yamaguchi, Lt Sada-o **71**
Yamanaka, PO1c Tadao **64**